CULTURALLY RELEVANT SCHOOLS

CREATING POSITIVE WORKPLACE RELATIONSHIPS AND PREVENTING INTERGROUP DIFFERENCES

JEAN A. MADSEN AND
REITUMETSE OBAKENG MABOKELA

ROUTLEDGE
NEW YORK AND LONDON

Published in 2005 by
Routledge
Taylor & Francis Group
270 Madison Avenue
New York, NY 10016

Published in Great Britain by
Routledge
Taylor & Francis Group
2 Park Square
Milton Park, Abingdon
Oxon OX14 4RN

© 2005 by Taylor & Francis Group
Routledge is an imprint of the Taylor & Francis Group

Printed in the United States of America on acid-free paper
10 9 8 7 6 5 4 3 2 1

International Standard Book Number-10: 0-415-94996-3 (Hardcover) 0-415-94997-1 (Softcover)
International Standard Book Number-13: 978-0-4159-4996-5 (Hardcover) 978-0-4159-4997-2
(Softcover)

Library of Congress Cataloging-in-Publication Data

Madsen, Jean.
  Culturally relevant schools : creating positive workplace relationships and preventing intergroup differences / Jean A. Madsen and Reitumetse Obakeng Mabokela.
     p. cm.
  Includes bibliographical references and index.
  ISBN 0-415-94996-3 (hb : alk. paper) — ISBN 0-415-94997-1 (pb : alk. paper)
  1. Multicultural education—United States. 2. School improvement programs—United States. 3. Educational sociology—United States. I. Mabokela, Reitumetse Obakeng. II. Title.
LC1099.3.M23 2005
370.117—dc22   2004023039

Taylor & Francis Group
is the Academic Division of T&F Informa plc.

Visit the Taylor & Francis Web site at
http://www.taylorandfrancis.com
and the Routledge Web site at
http://www.routledge-ny.com

I dedicate this book to my parents, Earl and Kay, who were generous with their support, modeled for me how to speak up for my beliefs, and taught me to respect everyone so I could cross racial lines.

Jean A. Madsen

For my son, Karabo, who has helped me to keep my perspective on the really important things in life; and my husband, Christopher Dunbar, Jr., whose love, support, and humor keep me grounded.

Reitumetse Obakeng Mabokela

Contents

VIII CONTENTS

Foreword

An interesting social phenomenon occurred during the latter half of the 20th century when white families exited the nation's cities in substantial numbers to move to the suburbs. This population shift, characterized by some observers as "white flight," was supposedly prompted by the desire for a "better quality of life." Following the civil rights movement, urban school systems tended to became more racially integrated, and one interpretation of the movement to the suburbs was that white parents did not want their children to have to attend schools where they would encounter substantial numbers of African American or Latino youngsters.

People of color have generally had limited access to suburban environments as a result of housing costs and zoning patterns, as well as prejudice and discrimination in acquiring mortgages and purchasing property. As a result, in great contrast to their urban counterparts, suburban schools tend to be predominantly white settings. Madsen and Mabokela have taken us inside these institutions and analyzed the interactions that occur there, focusing on students and teachers of color and the challenges that they must contend with. However, if schools are a metaphor for our society, then the importance of this research actually extends beyond those settings, because it illuminates the continuing deep-seated nature of the resistance to meaningful racial integration. We are reminded that most white Americans comfortably and conveniently exclude most people of color from their lives, and keep the ones who are allowed in on a very short leash.

Adaptation to the dominant culture is a fact of life for people of color. W.E.B. DuBois referred to this circumstance among African Americans as dual-consciousness: understanding and responding to the norms and values of white society while simultaneously maintaining and embracing their own cultural heritage. This quality seems to be manifested in teachers of color as they carry out their professional responsibilities in suburban schools. Notwithstanding their articulated appreciation of multiculturalism and diversity, suburban schools are revealed as settings that marginalize people of color. They minimize their perspectives and input, and pressure them to conform to the practices, styles, and attitudes of the majority.

In the 50 years since the landmark *Brown v. Board of Education* decision, the composition of suburban schools and the treatment of teachers and students of color within those schools remind us of how very far we have to travel as a nation. As the 21st century unfolds and brings with it the demographic reality of increasing numbers of people of color, it seems fitting to place the findings of Madsen and Mabokela into their appropriate context. That is to say, unless the covert resistance to integration is addressed, along with its resultant concentration of power, influence, and privilege in a limited portion of the population, then race, color, and culture will continue to be fundamental determinants of personal and professional worth in American society.

It is ironic that Madsen and Mabokela feel the need to offer a warning that their research findings may surprise or anger readers. This comment reflects the disturbing reality that Americans still do not face up to the prevalence of racist and discriminatory behavior that occurs everyday, both at the individual level and also through institutional structures. One could argue that the very existence of suburban communities as racial enclaves where white populations enjoy economic and social benefits that are denied to urban residents of color makes a mockery of the American ideals of equal opportunity and justice for all.

This volume is disturbing, precisely because it is revealing; it is important because it is hopeful. The authors conclude by presenting a strategic process through which diversity plans can be developed for schools. Clearly they are needed there, and in every other component of society as well. Suburban schools are the arenas where many of the leaders of the next generation are being prepared, and the attitudes of the students who come out of them must be congruent with the realities of the 21st century. These schools must develop a more inclusive ethos that not only tolerates, but truly celebrates diversity and multiculturalism.

William B. Harvey
American Council on Education

Acknowledgments

We would like to thank all the participants we interviewed for these studies. Countless African American and European American teachers, principals, and parents trusted us with their perceptions and experiences and spent their time with us. As a result of their participation, we could better understand workplace relationships and what they mean for preventing intergroup differences.

This work was collected over a period of time, so there are many people we want to acknowledge for their comments and support, including Etta Hollins, Randy Taylor, Robin Hughes, Barbara Taylor, and William Harvey. These individuals listened, read, and reread drafts of articles and chapters, suggested other references, and inspired us to continue.

In addition, we would like to thank our colleagues at Fontbonne College, University of Wisconsin-Milwaukee, Michigan State University, and Texas A&M University, who supported the collection and analysis of this research over a period of time. We also need to recognize our graduate assistants Jennifer Barrett, Nkrumah Dixon, and Yihsuan Chen, who helped with getting articles, copying data, and mailing manuscripts. Also, Marie, Bill, and Susan, who were always in the office to help us out. A great "thank you" to Sarah Wiseman for her outstanding editing of this manuscript. Also, thanks to Tom Madsen for your assistance with the copyediting.

We want to thank family and friends for their support in getting this work moved forward. In particular, I (Jean) would like to thank Jim,

Virginia, Joan, and John. Also, Dr. Melissa Powell, my advocate, who supported me through the completion of this book. And I want to thank my nieces and nephews for their humor; they motivate me to be better.

We acknowledge the support of Catherine Bernard and Brook Cosby at Routledge, who have supported our efforts from the very beginning to the completion of this book. I (Jean) thank Malcolm Clarkson, former editor at Falmer Press, who moved my career forward and has always supported me. Finally, a big "thank you" to Reitumetse (Reitu) for being such a great coauthor.

And thank you, Jean, for five years of a great collaborative partnership.

PREFACE

During the 50 years since the historic *Brown v. Board of Education* court decision, there has been great expectation that school desegregation will provide learning environments where children of color will thrive beyond the trappings of racially based restrictions. While there have been significant efforts and gains to create equitable academic environments, there is a disturbing reality that some of our schools continue to provide less than ideal learning conditions for our children, especially children of color. There are numerous accounts of poor rural schools, "at-risk" urban schools, children "left behind," the persistent performance gap between racial-ethnic minority students and their white peers, violent incidents, and myriad other disheartening episodes that negatively impact our children.

This book provides findings from research studies we have conducted to examine workplace relationships between African American teachers and European American participants in suburban school districts. To address issues of diversity in schools, we need to examine how people interact with others who are different from them and the implications of these interactions for creating positive exchanges and inclusive school cultures.

Culturally Relevant Schools aims to move the focus of diversity beyond the individual awareness phase to a more organizationally grounded approach. Rather than just promote the dialogue around diversity issues, we offer specific ideas for creating inclusive school environments that respond to pedagogical needs of diverse learners and provide a safe space where teachers can effectively engage and resolve issues of intergroup conflict.

Organization of the Book

Part I of this book is composed of three chapters that examine work-place relationships and their implications for the recruitment and retention of teachers of color. First, we present experiences of African American teachers in suburban school contexts and explore how school culture impacts the ways the participants respond to, and engage with, diversity-related issues. Our findings reveal that African American teachers often experience heightened scrutiny of their professional (and sometimes personal) activities, alienation if they do not conform to the prescribed culture, and role entrapment that limits their contribution to addressing issues related to diversity. In many ways, schools that have overly prescriptive majority cultures lead racial-ethnic minority teachers to establish "protective hesitation," to protect their own sense of cultural identity and professional integrity.

Dickens and Dickens (1991) contend that people of color face multiple obstacles when they enter a majority organization. Our research indicates that African Americans experience a one-way adaptation of their school culture. That is, there is an expectation that the teachers will embrace the norms, values, beliefs, and culture of their schools without question. Yet, there is little consideration of how the presence of African American teachers might impact the school.

Chapter 2 examines intergroup differences and group boundaries and their impact on professional experiences of African American teachers. The African American teachers in our study often are the only or one of very few teachers of color within their schools. This chronic underrepresentation creates an environment where they are treated as perpetual visitors. That is, majority teachers very subtly establish group boundaries that serve as "constant reminders of difference."

Chapter 3 highlights the problems of role entrapment for African American teachers. The majority culture in suburban schools forces these teachers to fit preexisting generalizations that confine them to limited roles within the organization. Our African American teachers confronted multiple barriers in establishing their place within suburban schools. One obstacle highlights the treatment of cultural difference as a weakness. Because there were so few teachers of color in these contexts, the African American teachers were relegated to the "Black expert" role, resulting in isolation and their being perceived as "affirmative action hires." Furthermore, this role entrapment and ineffective use of their talents and expertise seriously compromised their ability to pursue professional positions beyond their narrowly defined roles.

We contend that to improve the organizational culture, it is imperative to reduce intergroup conflict. The three chapters in part II examine how leaders in diverse contexts must understand their important role in addressing intergroup conflict. Leadership and diversity are invariably connected, and may be used effectively as "agents of influence" to prevent and to manage difference and conflict. In chapters 4 and 5, we examine how two different ethnic groups of leaders perceived and responded to intergroup differences in their schools. The European American principals in chapter 4 highlighted the inadequacy of their preparation to appropriately engage with and respond to diversity-related issues. Because of the few teachers of color in these principals' schools, the European American principals indicated that they placed the responsibility (and sometimes the burden) of addressing diversity issues on these individuals. They saw the teachers of color as the change agents, yet gave them little authority and support to implement policies and procedures that would create meaningful changes within their schools. Because of these principals' inability to address effectively intergroup tensions stemming from diversity-related issues, teacher subgroups and racial boundaries emerged, further stigmatizing the place and value of difference within these schools.

African American leaders in chapter 5 expressed intergroup differences similar to those of their European American counterparts, but responded differently. They developed a "color-conscious" approach to ensure equitable practices for all children. The African American administrators provided insights on what skills are needed to understand how to deal with intergroup differences. They were able to move between the cultural identities and incorporate the connections and interrelationships among the groups. Consequently, their school participants benefited because these administrators were responsible for dispelling stereotypes and proving themselves as competent leaders.

In chapter 6 we make a case for diversity self-efficacy as a strategy for dealing with intergroup differences. Leaders need to feel efficacious in their ability to address intergroup differences. Therefore, they need to be more than just aware about diverse groups; they need to be trained in order to gain the confidence and the capabilities to regulate and direct their behaviors toward managing racial difference in schools.

Part III provides some exploratory solutions schools may consider to create culturally responsive schools. In chapters 7 and 8 we present leadership skills that are essential for leaders who work in diverse contexts, and we offer a strategic diversity plan process for the effective management of difference and creation of inclusive school cultures. Chapter 7 provides a framework of essential leadership skills for effective management within diverse contexts. Central to the process of effective diversity leadership is the leader's capacity to understand his or her own cultural identity and its impact on leadership behavior; to implement a relational identity orientation to promote interpersonal cooperation and create integrated networks among and between school participants; and to establish an organizational structure that adapts to the changing needs of diverse students, teachers, and community participants.

In the final chapter we propose the development of a strategic diversity plan, a process that has been used in the corporate sector to manage diversity issues. We certainly do not advocate an unproblematic adoption of this process, but it does offer an alternative approach to effective management of diversity within our schools. In diverse contexts, it is critical to create an adaptable structure that evolves and expands as a diverse population enters the school doors. We believe that the tensions between the traditional structure and the development of participatory principles may be addressed through a strategic process. A diversity proposal assists leaders with ways to examine how the school recruits and retains teachers, socializes teachers upon their entry into a diverse context, and creates teaming structures to represent heterogeneous groupings. In addition, this process provides ways for administrators to motivate and reward individuals who do well in working with their diverse student population. A strategic effort is one approach that leaders may employ to remove barriers so all individuals may become effective contributors within their schools.

PART I

WORKPLACE
RELATIONSHIPS AND
INTERGROUP DIFFERENCES

Due to the presence of diversity in schools, attention should be given on how these contexts can promote social norms for cohesiveness and mutual understanding. In creating such settings, differences between people are explained as plausible and valid alternative customs, traditions, and points of view. Therefore, participants support each other as they begin to understand and appreciate the validation of alternative points of view and establish social norms that allow them to become interdependent. This interdependence creates the processes by which people form the social norms that facilitate positive working conditions. Thus, inclusiveness is derived from a supportive environment that affirms diversity as an explicit value.

We have chosen to illuminate the experiences of students and teachers of color in suburban schools. This environment is not usually associated with problems that plague many poor rural or "at-risk" urban schools, but our research shows that it harbors a set of challenges that may be detrimental to students and teachers of color if left unaddressed. In part I of this book, we examine workplace relationships and their implications for the recruitment and retention of teachers of color in suburban contexts. Few studies have been completed that truly examine the attitudes and beliefs behind how teachers of color cope and survive in these challenging school contexts. The first three chapters shed light on how the African American teachers in our study negotiated issues related to performance pressures, group boundaries and intergroup differences, and role entrapment. Each chapter provides insights on how these teachers perceived their school contexts and developed strategies for improving their workplace environment.

School Organization and Implications for Teachers of Color

The personal experiences and professional education of teachers affect the routines and knowledge of African American teachers within their school environment (Porter & Brophy, 1988). For teachers of color to be acculturated into a European American school, they have to acquire the necessary socialization patterns to understand their European American colleagues' codes of power. Teachers of color are often excluded and scrutinized by European American teachers who have had minimal exposure to non-Anglo norms and values (Frierson, 1990). When schools are based on the normative notions of a European American culture, how do teachers of color in these cultural contexts assert their own values and beliefs?

Cox (1994) contends that organizations need to understand how various group identities within the workplace impact intergroup differences and affect the culture of organizations. He asserts that both phenotype identities (physical and observable differences of groups) and cultural group identities (shared norms and common social heritage) influence how various ethnic groups will interact with the dominant culture. In traditional, assimilation-oriented organizations, members of phenotype groups that are different from the dominant group will have less favorable work experiences and career outcomes than persons from the dominant group. Within phenotype groups, there will be an inverse relationship between the degree of distinctiveness in physical attributes and career outcome.

The culture within an organization greatly influences how minorities will be treated by their European American counterparts. Strong organizational cultures provide cues on how to behave and establish reinforcing expectations to influence members (Cox, 1994). In these dominant organizational cultures, minorities are required to conform to the values and norms of the majority culture while having limited opportunities to assert their own beliefs. Because the majority establishes work norms, it institutes rules and regulations that people of color are expected to obey.

Smart and St. John (1996) believe that strong organizational cultures are effective when there is congruence between the espoused beliefs and actual practices. While many organizations may promote a commitment to hiring minorities, some are unwilling to support or facilitate minority members' transition to a majority organization. Cose's (1993) research notes that even if minorities are able to fit within the organization, they are never seen as individuals but as stereotypes of racial groups. Jablin (1987) asserts that small-scale socialization is often difficult for people of color to learn and to maintain. Often, minorities in dominant organizations do not have access to the informal networks that tend to develop in the workplace. As a result, many minorities feel isolated and believe that they are treated differently from their majority counterparts. Some people of color indicated that they are often excluded from social activities, have their work scrutinized, are given misinformation, and are sabotaged in their work efforts by majority workers (Morrison, 1996).

A school's organizational culture establishes how its participants will approach issues of diversity. Thus, school norms and their cultural nuances establish the work climate that will accommodate and lead to greater flexibility on diversity-related issues. Schools need to understand how gender, race, national origin, and work specialization create microculture groups. They need to understand how subgroups inevitably help determine the school culture. Suburban desegregated schools often deal with microculture groups by exerting strong pressure on teachers of color to assimilate to the existing culture. Beause of these pressures, teachers of color may establish a cultural distance from the prevailing school norms or have to modify their behavior in order to achieve acceptance (Cox, 2001). Although such schools ostensibly do nothing to change their culture, and in fact work very hard to reassert it, the added dynamic of pressuring a certain group is itself a major change in the schools' social climate. It is not enough simply to hire teachers of color as the way to achieve diversity. For diversity to flourish, it is crucial to develop a school's organizational capacity to leverage diversity as a resource. To develop dynamically with diversity as a valued input should be the challenge for schools. Hence, it is imperative that in recruiting teachers of color, we create conditions in which performance barriers are minimized, and enhance the potential for all to learn about diversity-related issues.

As people of color enter a dominant organizational culture, they go through what Dickens and Dickens (1991) call a developmental process of survival and success. Dickens and Dickens interviewed successful Black managers in predominantly white organizations to ascertain how they triumphed over many obstacles. Based on their interviews, they determined that these Black managers went through four phases of development: (1) entry phase, (2) adjusting phase, (3) planned growth phase, and (4) success phase. They designated these developmental phases as a closed-loop model because each time a person of color is promoted or reassigned, the cycle begins again. However, they found that each time this occurs, it takes a shorter time to traverse each phase. Furthermore, Dickens and Dickens believe that time spent in each phase varies because of individual differences and is characterized by different attitudes, emotions, behavior, and job skills.

The initial phase of entry and survival requires people of color to deal with a range of emotions from confusion about their interactions with majority workers to feeling a strong need to fit in (Dickens & Dickens, 1991). Also during this initial phase they go through an adjusting process of testing the organization. Many times during this period, people of color see their majority peers given more responsibility while they themselves feel no growth or personal job satisfaction. In addition, they undergo considerable stress with regard to the way their job performance is assessed. In many ways these individuals are concerned about how they fit into the "normal" corporate organization and how they will socialize and interact with majority workers who have had little or no exposure to racial minorities; they wonder if they will be given adequate support to complete their responsibilities and whether they will feel as educated and competent as their counterparts.

The second phase focuses on planned growth and success within the organization (Dickens & Dickens, 1991). During the planned growth period, people of color make a conscious and concerted effort to expand their abilities to be adaptable and improve their personal development. Thus, they become "superstars," exerting more energy than their counterparts. They acquire a sense of determination and use their anger as a strategy to remove the barriers under their own control, and learn to make the proper demands on their organization in order to advance. Dickens and Dickens (1991) believe that during the planned growth period, in every interaction with their white counterparts, there is always a racial component. Thus, during this phase people of color soon realize they need to accept this fact, plan for it, and manage accordingly.

In the success phase, managers of color become aware of additional burdens with which they must deal (Dickens & Dickens, 1991). While they are viewed positively by their majority counterparts for their productive attitudes and work efforts, some of them become concerned with how they will be viewed by others of their cultural group (Dickens & Dickens, 1991). Validated by their majority peers, they now worry about how they will be perceived by those higher up the corporate ladder while also worrying about whether they will retain their sense of cultural identity and feeling responsible for and obligated to other people of color in subordinate positions. In this phase, Black managers can look outward, but they still need to be aware of prejudiced behavior around them and to use peripheral vision in their interactions with others (Dickens & Dickens, 1991).

Given the research on the developmental stages for people of color entering majority organizations, what are the implications for teachers of color in suburban desegregated schools? Dickens and Dickens's participants were successful Black managers who had received validation from their majority counterparts. The African American teachers who were interviewed never said they ever felt they could let their guard down while in these contexts, nor did they feel a sense of support from their majority school participants. While these African American teachers reflected developmental stages similar to Dickens and Dickens's stages, they were never able to move beyond protective hesitation, a coping mechanism in which they felt the need to protect themselves from the psychological scrutiny they experienced when interacting with European American school participants.

In the research presented in this section of the book, we provide a closer examination of the obstacles of performance pressure, intergroup differences, and role entrapment that may have prevented some of the participants from reaching the "success" phase. Subjected to the performance pressure of always being scrutinized in all of their actions, these African American teachers never felt a sense of psychic well-being, which resulted in their isolating themselves. In their interactions with European American teachers, group boundaries and intergroup differences resulted, creating tensions in these contexts. Because of the strong organizational culture in these suburban desegregated contexts, the African American teachers were expected to use traditional instructional practices and remain "color-blind" when African American students were disciplined unfairly. Finally, these African American teachers became trapped in a role: their advice was sought only on "Black" issues, preventing them from being perceived as successful in their classrooms. Consequently, the workplace relationships in these contexts created tensions for teachers of color that have serious implications not only for recruiting teachers but for retaining them as well.

The research findings presented in the next three chapters may surprise or anger readers who are not fully aware of how institutional and personal prejudices can influence the numbers of teachers of color in these contexts. We ask that you try to understand rather than react. We hope our findings provide some explanation of what actually happens to teachers of color who begin teaching in suburban desegregated schools. If we really consider attracting and retaining teachers of color in majority schools a priority, we must value the important contributions that these individuals bring to the classroom. We must strive to create a culture that supports them in moving through all of Dickens and Dickens's developmental stages, a culture that perceives itself as thereby nourishing itself.

Overview of Chapters

Part I is composed of three chapters that examine workplace relationships and their implications for the recruitment and retention of teachers of color. These chapters present descriptive analyses that examine how the organizational culture of predominantly white schools and the cultural values that African American teachers bring into these schools affect the latter's professional experiences in schools where they are in the minority. The theoretical premise for the findings discussed in these chapters emerges from Cox's (1994) research on group identities. His work was used as a broad overview to examine how workers from phenotype groups define themselves, as well as how other groups view them.

In addition to Cox, our theoretical framework is informed by two other studies that examine issues of minority group identity within a majority organization: Cose's (1993) study of African Americans employed in majority organizations and Kanter's (1977) study of women in predominantly male organizations. Cose's study revealed that African Americans encountered difficult working environments that interfered with their well-being and their ability to position themselves within the organization. Many of these African Americans left their jobs because of the difficulties they faced working in organizations dominated by European Americans. Kanter's research on women employed in mostly European American male organizations revealed that they had to cope with performance pressures that led to their entrapment within the organization.

In the first chapter, we examine the performance pressures that the African American teachers experienced within their suburban school environment and how they developed defense mechanisms to cope with their isolation and the perpetual scrutiny of their abilities. The second chapter highlights the significance of intergroup differences for the pedagogical practices of African Americans and their European American counterparts. Cultural differences created boundaries that emerged in the areas of discipline, misperceptions of students of color, and professional exchanges. While the school culture supported more traditional pedagogical practices, these practices were not responsive to the academic needs of students of color. The third chapter reveals the entrapment of African American teachers in the role of the "Black expert." In this situation the professional expertise of the African American teachers is limited to dealing with issues related to minority concerns.

1

PERFORMANCE PRESSURES AND AUTOMATIC NOTICE

Introduction

Tensions of intergroup conflict become apparent if there are only one or a few teachers of color in the entire school. Our analysis reveals the entrapment of African American teachers in the role of the "Black expert." That is, the professional expertise of the African American teachers was boxed in, confining them to dealing with issues that related to minority concerns. African American teachers are subjected to performance pressures when they are expected to be the sole respondent on "Black issues" and when they are encouraged to respond only to those issues and no others; thus they bear the burden of taking action on issues based on race and not on their ability to teach. Because of their high visibility as the only teacher or one of very few teachers of color in their school, these teachers experience intergroup tensions that impact their work experiences and their relationships with European American teachers.

Our findings highlight strategies these African American teachers employed to negotiate the institutional culture of their schools and, more significantly, the pivotal role that the school leader (principal) plays in how teachers of color are treated in these schools. School leaders need to use their positions of authority to create an organizational culture that supports and alleviates the challenging working conditions that teachers of color face in suburban school contexts.

Intergroup Theory and Performance Pressures

We employed intergroup theory and Kanter's (1977) research on performance pressures to understand how the members of the dominant culture who have had little exposure to others who are ethnically different from them often exert performance pressures on teachers of color in suburban desegregated schools. Intergroup theory explains how individual identity and diverse groups interact within a larger organizational context (Nkomo & Cox, 1996). Key elements of intergroup theory are relevant to issues of diversity that may impact (1) the circumstances that lead to the formation of groups, their boundaries, roles, and development cycle; (2) the effect of individual and group membership and the intergroup dynamics in dealing with prejudices; and (3) recognition of the problems of identity, power, conflict, and social comparisons in groups (Watts, 1994).

Kanter's (1977) framework identified three perceptual tendencies that impact the way underrepresented individuals are perceived within organizations in which they are in the minority. The first perceptual tendency is that "tokens" have higher visibility than majority workers do. As a result, "tokens" are subject to performance pressures to ensure that they maintain the normative cues of the organization. Polarization or exaggeration of differences is the second perceptual tendency. The presence of a person bearing a different set of characteristics makes members of a majority group more aware both of their commonalities with and their differences from the "token." There is a tendency to exaggerate the extent of these differences, especially because underrepresented individuals are too few in number to prevent the application of familiar generalizations or stereotypes. Assimilation, the third perceptual tendency, reflects the stereotypical assumptions about "tokens" that lead to status leveling and role entrapment.

Because of the high visibility of these African American teachers, Kanter's (1977) research was useful in defining the performance pressures that the African American teachers encountered in these contexts. Kanter's first perceptual tendency, performance pressures, identified three factors. The first, automatic notice, is a proportional rarity of "tokens" that results in a one-by-one examination in which underrepresented individuals capture a larger awareness share. Thus, the actions of people who are ethnically different are overly scrutinized. "Symbolic consequences" refers to the burden persons of color may encounter in representing who they are in the context. The final category is fighting discrepant qualities; a person's accomplishments are often overshadowed as a result of negative reactions to their mere presence in the workplace.

Given that Kanter's study is based on European American women, it is limited in explaining the racial undertones voiced by the African American teachers in this study. Cose (1993) and Anderson (1999) provide an additional theoretical basis to describe the discriminatory experiences that African Americans face in majority organizations. Cose (1993) interviewed African Americans employed in professional settings who encountered racism that interfered with their psychological well-being and their ability to position themselves within the organization. His interviews revealed that many African Americans often experienced the "dozen demons" that impact African Americans' psychological well-being. Resonating with the experiences of Cose's participants was Anderson's (1999) research as he interviewed African Americans in majority group organizations. His study revealed that African Americans must deal with complex social dynamics in their interactions with their European American colleagues.

Few studies addressing issues of diversity at the organizational level have been conducted in schools. Cox (2001) contends that the organizational diversity research conducted in corporations has generalizabilty to nonprofit organizations and, in particular, to schools. The debate about how schools are viewed as organizations creates tensions between whether schools are communities or bureaucracies. It does, however, reflect a perspective that indicates the organizational dimensions of schools (Verdugo, Greenberg, Henderson, Uribe, & Schneider, 1997). Because of the limited number of organizational diversity research studies conducted in schools, we make the connections to schools as organizations in order to reflect the complexity of intergroup dynamics among diverse groups in schools and to understand how teachers of color respond to and deal with performance pressures in these environments.

Performance Pressures

In dealing with performance pressures, the African American teachers in our study had developed defense mechanisms to cope with their isolation and the perpetual scrutiny of their abilities. They identified various performance pressures in their work environment, the first three being expressed along Kanter's dimensions: (1) issues with automatic notice; (2) symbolic consequences; and (3) fighting discrepant stereotypes and qualities. A fourth dimension, which we call "cultural switching," also emerged from our conversations with our participants. Because of these teachers' high visibility, these four pressures illuminate the crux of their experiences. Both male and female teachers identified similar experiences, but there were subtle differences in their response patterns. These factors may include different teaching levels of the participants, cultural backgrounds, gender issues, and varying personalities. The following discussion reflects these African American teachers' perceptions of how they responded to the performance pressures they experienced in their suburban schools.

Automatic Notice

Kanter (1977) contends that the automatic notice of "tokens" results in their becoming the subject of conversation, gossip, and careful scrutiny. Anderson (1999) states that in organizations, skin color is the persistent issue and a conspicuous and observable characteristic that makes individuals subject to negative consideration and treatment. The teachers in this study reported that they were highly visible within their schools. This automatic notice made it apparent to the African American participants that their majority colleagues were held to different standards, and they were expected to perform under conditions that were different from the ones the European American teachers experienced. The African American teachers believed that their small representation at these schools led to their being overly scrutinized. They felt that all of their actions were public, and everything they did in their classrooms was examined by their European American counterparts. Thus, being automatically noticed by their colleagues resulted in their feeling that their achievements would be limited (Cose, 1993).

Analysis of the data revealed that while both the male and female teachers experienced automatic notice, they responded differently. The female African American teachers expressed greater reliance on their cultural identity as a way to cope with automatic notice. They stated that the impact of automatic notice was more than they could bear at times. In contrast, the male African American teachers expressed the need to be self-disciplined and to take control by reacting to automatic notice in a competitive manner. This resulted in the male teachers being less negative about their peers' scrutiny than the female teachers were.

The male teachers perceived the stress of automatic notice as a positive factor that pushed them competitively. They responded to their peers' scrutiny as an impetus to compete against their European American colleagues. These male participants generated an energy that grew more internalized the longer they remained at their schools. It became apparent that the more experienced among them learned over time that automatic notice meant higher expectations. The less experienced males, however, felt the need to have some control over their peers' scrutiny of their presence.

The four male respondents who had been at their schools the longest noted the pressures of automatic notice. On the other hand, they perceived that this type of scrutiny was to be expected. They felt school leaders were responsible for exerting these pressures, and that they were expected to be better than the European American teachers were. One participant called this performance pressure the "Jackie Robinson syndrome." That is, as the only African American male teacher in his school, he perceived that he would have to work harder than his colleagues because his performance was under constant examination. Automatic notice, furthermore, meant having to prove that one was a qualified, competent teacher who deserved a position within the school system. The male teachers offered the following observations:

> When I first came here, I really got the feeling that there were people who were expecting me to fail. I had never failed. There

was no chance of me failing. I am a successful professional with a very impressive track record. I have sufficient evidence that indicates there was a "standoffishness" of me [by the European American teachers] to prove myself. People weren't so generous in helping me when I got here. There were instances where people could have been supportive and spared me some anguish, but they failed to when they knew that they could have. But it did not matter significantly, because I have been successful.

Another teacher concurred:

I'm 53, and I guess, having the experiences that I've had, I've learned that you have to be yourself. You can't get stressed out. It's true for a lot of minorities, if you are going to a place, you are the only one or two. I think a lot of people feel the pressure. I'm at the stage I don't care about that. I've been successful. I am not carrying the baggage anymore of having to be the "best of" because of what I am. I am a teacher.

Many of the male participants indicated they had to control the pressures in their work environment. Two male teachers who had been at their schools for approximately 7 years defined "control of the pressure" as being self-disciplined, remaining positive, and learning to disregard their intolerant colleagues. They accepted the pressures from the European Americans and enacted their own version of how to respond to this orientation. One participant said that he accepted being the "token" in order to overcompensate and to justify his worthiness at every opportunity.

Furthermore, these less experienced male teachers cited the lack of support from their European American peers, which left them to question their decision to remain at the school. Unlike the veteran participants, these male teachers felt that rather than just let the pressure occur, they needed to be in charge of how they were perceived by their European American colleagues. In essence, they turned the automatic notice into strategies that allowed them to retain their sense of identity and have power over their work environment. While these male participants learned to deal with automatic notice, they were still bothered by their peers' perceptions that they were unqualified. One of them noted:

> When I first got here, I felt that the teachers felt that I was not up to par. I did pick that up in their comments. I think one [European American] teacher called me "culturally deprived." He offered me an opportunity to come over to his house and go to church or something. There were several [European American] teachers who were brought in at the same time as me. I just noted the differences in the way we were treated. We were the same age, young people, first job, and so forth. I just noticed the assistance they got and I had to fend for myself. In general there was a perception and that pressure that kept me here to 8 P.M.

Interestingly, only one of the male participants noted that he did not "buy into" the pressures of being "superteacher." Of all of the male participants, he was the only one who did not want to recognize automatic notice as influencing his work. Yet, he believed that if he was prepared well for the teaching profession, he would not have to worry about the scrutiny that came with being the "token." His response regarding automatic notice did not seem to fit with those of the other male participants:

> The pressure to be "superteacher," I can't buy into that. It seems to me you need to go in there and do your job. And I think if you go in there and do the things you are supposed to do, the things you were trained to do, you're going to be fine. My pressure is trying to turn this off on Saturdays and Sundays so I can have somewhat of a life, because it drains you so. That's the pressure I have. Not the pressure that I'm going to do a good job. The pressure for me isn't in the performance; the pressure is in the preparation to perform. It's not external, but internal.

In sharp contrast, the female African American teachers responded negatively to automatic notice and resented the overexposure. They viewed automatic notice as very harmful and mentioned coping strategies in response to public pressures. One of their strategies was the need to have a strong reference-group orientation in which there was a reliance on a strong support system outside the school and the ability to connect to their cultural identity. The African American teachers' conceptualization of cultural identity aligns with Cox's (1994) research, in which he conceives of this idea as two-pronged: "cultural identity profile" refers to the culture group(s) with which an individual identifies, while "identity strength" refers to the significance that an individual places on a given cultural group. These interrelated prongs constitute the essence of the sense of cultural identity for these teachers. By having a strong cultural identity, they were able to filter out prejudices and deal with the low expectations that permeated their interactions with their European American colleagues.

Throughout the interviews, the female teachers openly stated that their sense of who they were and a connection to their community was important in dealing with automatic notice. Cross, Strauss, and Fhagen-Smith (1999) believe that as African Americans learn to immerse themselves in another group's experiences, they develop bridging competencies that allow them to function, yet do not suppress their sense of "Blackness." That is, the female teachers found a way to draw upon their cultural identity and were able to deflect the discomfort of being the only African American teacher in their building.

The female participants with 5 to 10 years of experience relied heavily on their cultural identity as a security factor and were not intimidated by the normative structure of the school. Consequently, the more experienced female teachers stated that the longer they remained in their schools, the stronger they became in their cultural identity and the less able they were to remain race neutral in responding to students of color. These internalized strategies helped these female teachers to retain their cultural identity and to buffer those colleagues who at times challenged their competency as teachers. A female African American teacher's comment illustrates this point:

> The strange thing is, when you think of yourself, you have these labels. My label is I am a Black woman. Sometimes it's harder dealing with the fact that because I am Black in an all-white school, I am dealt with differently. I see the difference of having taught in an all-Black school that I need to feel secure enough about my self-image that I don't have to cat-walk down the street. I don't have to talk like I don't belong when I am here.

My feelings still get hurt being here, but the environment I was raised in was so nurturing that once you get out of it, you are strong enough. You have to be secure enough about yourself and that the standards you are setting are standards that not only are appropriate for your kids, but for all kids. You have to have a level of confidence that you have to pass on not only to your minority students, but to the other students as well.

The one female teacher who had been at her school for less than a year cited her strong sense of cultural identity as a baseline to retain her confidence. It was apparent that she was aware of her sense of cultural identity but had not internalized these bridging functions. Unlike the other African American teachers, she was unsure if the European American teachers and students would accept her. She was troubled at her inability to move back and forth in order to balance her cultural identity with the expectations that the school held for her. She felt confined by the perceptions of the European American teachers and was uncomfortable being herself. A comparison of the first-year teacher's comments with those of the female participants with 7 to 10 years of experience revealed her inability to refine her self-defense mechanisms and to negotiate the school's organizational culture. She reflected:

> The other day I was really loud and I thought, "I'm that typical Black person." I am just trying to be myself. I am always saying to myself, "Don't lose your identity when you get out there." I start doing that. People then say that's typical; that's how people act. You see, that's one of the reasons why I sometimes can't be myself, because I just want to be loose. It's kind of hard because then you want to watch yourself to make sure you're not being loud or have white people say that's how Black people act.

Symbolic Consequences

Symbolic consequences refers to the pressure placed upon minority group members to become representatives of their race in response to the stereotypical beliefs of their majority peers, and the treatment that follows from that stereotyped portrayal. As Kanter (1977) indicated, because of the visibility of underrepresented individuals in the workplace, majority workers attempt to categorize them according to their stereo-typical views about members of minority groups. When these individu-als do not represent the majority's perceptions of a specific minority group, the person of color acquires an elevated status. Thus, the person of color is not viewed as a true representation of his or her race. Cose (1993) further indicates that most organizations seek specific assurances that the people of color they hire have qualities that will enable them, despite their color, to blend into the traditional beliefs of the school. Thus, the pressures of representing their race and their ability to blend in created stressful conditions for these African American teachers.

The most conflicting expectation that the participants encountered was that their European American colleagues did not perceive them as being true "African Americans." They stated that their peers felt they did not fit the African American stereotypes portrayed in the media. As a result of this misrepresentation, both the male and female African American teachers believed they were expected to accept the traditional structure of the school norms and hold beliefs like those of their Euro-pean American colleagues. The following comment captured the essence of the male and female African American teachers' encounters with their peers:

> The other people [European American colleagues] are mono-cultural. I have had enough white associations. They are the ones that have few Black associations. I am the novelty to them. They are not different from me. I am different from them. I get tired of that. Interestingly enough, the other three Black teach-ers here, we are four different people. Sometimes I wonder if my white colleagues realize how different we are. Each of us grew up in a different part of the country, our backgrounds are differ-ent, there are age differentials, general temperament, and inter-ests. I can establish a common ground, but it is not easy, given the fact that we are so different.

In an effort to negotiate the organizational culture and structure, these teachers reported, they had to be careful about the racial implica-tions of their associations with European American teachers. It is in this intergroup dynamics that confusion and frustration arise for minority workers who appear either "too white" or "too Black" in their professional or social exchanges with majority workers (Anderson, 1999). Participants struggled with how to remain true to their race without appearing to compromise their cultural identities. They believed, furthermore, that their European American counterparts were ambivalent about their presence; hence, these African American teachers felt that they could not compromise themselves and that they could not back down from issues that arose from the desegregation program.

There were differences between the more experienced male and female African American teachers and the participants with fewer years of experience in how they responded to pressures of symbolic consequences. The older and more experienced African American teachers often isolated themselves and reduced their contact with European American teachers. The collective reaction from these more experienced teachers was to let their anger go and remain silent. To them, it was not in their best interest to be combative. However, the more experienced females did state that at times, not often, they addressed racial inequities at their schools.

Interestingly, the older male African American participants who experienced the explicit racism of the 1950s and 1960s stated that nothing they encountered in their school was as challenging as what they had faced growing up. These teachers indicated that the experiences of growing up during the turbulent 1960s, when race relations were hostile, developed their resilience to racial incidents. In addition, these males believed it was more important for them not to let European American teachers intimidate them. One older male noted:

> There never was a time I felt the racial pressures that were exerted on me in this district would be of major intensity enough to make me turn and run. By the time I got to this district, I had been bathed in some of the best racial fires there were. I mean, coming from Mississippi, I had no illusions about what lurked sometimes behind smiles and faces of people we meet. I was tougher than most people who tried to intimidate me. I had no illusions about what I was, who I was. Of course, in the early days, I walked a tightrope and stayed out of situations that would cause anyone to arch their eyebrows in my direction. You're concerned about your image. It's only after you get older,

where I am in life, that you're more defiant. That's an attitude you can only get by being successful for a time and taking your place among your colleagues, establishing your place.

Much like the veteran males, the experienced female African American teachers became socially disengaged. Unlike their male counterparts, however, they no longer "bite their tongues" during faculty meetings when disparaging comments are made about African American students. The female African American teachers acknowledged that while they made attempts to distance themselves from other faculty members, they continued to be advocates for the African American students. Thus, the female African American teachers who remained in their schools developed finely tuned defense mechanisms, such as withdrawing when the emotional costs were too high. This quote succinctly captures these more experienced female teachers' perspective:

> At lunchtimes I sit in my own room. I have a refrigerator and a microwave in my room. I just mainly want silence from teachers. So I close the door and heat up my lunch and have 30 minutes to myself. I guess they do say insensitive things. The reason I don't eat lunch with them is that I don't like discussing students [the African American students] over lunch. I don't like to be negative. Because I keep myself positive, I can function. I like to exercise, listen to music, and I like to go to a movie. I just can't do it if I am washed out. Then I have to go home and go to bed. I've learned how to pick my battles, then how to withdraw to maintain my sanity.

It became evident to these veteran teachers that in order to remain in these schools, they had to understand how they were or were not appropriately perceived by their colleagues. In response to their symbolic representations, these veteran male and female African American teachers preferred to identify themselves as persons with more general roles than just being the "Black expert" who was hired to teach students of color. These participants learned early in their tenure that they were hired to represent other African Americans. These teachers felt compromised by this narrow definition of their expertise and disliked their role as "tokens." As a result, some of the veteran teachers felt demoralized and cynical, and expressed concerns about their value in the school. As a way to continue in their work, they often isolated themselves socially and professionally.

In contrast, the younger teachers responded to their European American peers differently. They retained positive attitudes about their value and role in their schools. This optimistic outlook was important because it enhanced their perceptions about themselves and their work in these contexts. It also meant that they had some control over their destiny in the school. These less experienced teachers believed that by presenting themselves as approachable, they could form positive relationships with their European American colleagues. The African American teachers believed it was important for them to provide their European American colleagues with an understanding of how their stereotypes and narrow views were problematic for students of color. While they were willing to assist the European American faculty, they also realized the potential problems if they became too verbal or assertive. These less experienced participants walked a tightrope of balancing their place at the school with the need to respond to the needs of the students of color. This quote from a less experienced African American teacher summarizes the situation:

> I think the people here wonder what the hell I am going to say. I don't think I am perceived as the average Black person in terms of how to relate and so forth. But at the same time, for a person who's going to be outspoken or sensitive in terms of what they will think sort of prohibits some of the nonsense questions that are asked [by coworkers]. So becoming too political or something like that is perceived as somehow threatening for Black teachers, since the perception is that you don't bring up Black issues. People feel very uncomfortable dealing with Black issues.

The differences in how to approach their colleagues about issues of race was more problematic for the less experienced male teachers. Because these participants felt the need to dispel stereotypes about African American males, they were concerned with how they were perceived by their European American colleagues. The less experienced males felt that if they remained quiet when racist comments were

made, their silence or lack of reaction reinforced opportunities for more
racially insensitive comments to be allowed. Yet, if they were vocal,
they jeopardized their chances to improve conditions for children of
color. These male teachers expressed conflict over how best to respond
to their colleagues' comments, and they were uncertain about the most
effective approach. The need to dispel "African American male" stereotypes was often the reason they gave for the ways they responded to
their European American peers' questions and concerns.

In contrast, the less experienced female participants stated that they
ignored racial slurs that often were made in faculty meetings and other
social contexts. They acknowledged that they continued to address
prejudices that occurred in their schools. Furthermore, these female
teachers believed that it was better to model instructional practices for
their peers than to engage in a dialogue about teaching. These less
experienced female teachers noted that they often thought through
their decisions on whether to challenge their colleagues or ignore them.
They were more willing to disregard their coworkers' racially motivated
questions and bear the burden of hearing complaints about teaching
children of color. This quote from a less experienced female reflects
their situation:

> So it's been a lot of different things, a lot of paths to cross, a lot
> of times where I had to grit my teeth, grin and bear it, and just
> go on. But I felt like, going back to my first year, if I didn't stay,
> then I couldn't make a way for someone else. So ethnic jokes
> started to spread, and then people felt comfortable. I became
> invisible to them at times, and they wanted to say something
> about this Black person. Often, they [European American col-
> leagues] went with a negative term and I would call attention to
> it. So I had to assert myself to get more respect and make sure I
> didn't do it in a combative way. It offends me greatly.

Of all of the participants, the first-year female teacher struggled
the most with how to respond to her colleagues' comments. She was
unable to handle the stereotypical questions about African Americans.
She stated on several occasions that she often felt that the European
American teachers tried to intimidate her. This first-year teacher questioned her decision to remain at the school. She talked about how her

principal made her feel incompetent when she accidentally sent a paper home with a sticker placed upside down. Unlike the other participants, she never discussed any strategies she employed to deal with low expectations and the anger from the European American teachers that she was an affirmative-action hire. As the year progressed, she eventually gained enough confidence to state her issues with her colleagues and students' parents. She recalled in her interview:

> She was one of my more boisterous parents. I think she wanted to intimidate me. I mean, the night before, I was just so upset with these teachers and parents that I just cried to myself. I pulled myself together and told them that if they did not like the way I teach, I'm sorry. I think they really wanted to get me to a point where they could tell me what to do and how to do it. My principal told me she would support me, but she pulled a child out of my class. But then she [the principal] told me she was not pulling any more children from my class. In a way, I wish that she had just pulled them out, and that would be one less headache for me.

Throughout our interviews, the African American teachers cited problems of dealing with public scrutiny and the symbolic consequences of representing their race. It was apparent that they underwent personal stress and expended considerable energy to maintain productive personal and professional relationships with their European American colleagues. The longer these teachers remained at the school, the more they developed defense strategies that were meant to isolate them and limit their contacts with European American teachers. As Dickens and Dickens (1991) noted, entry into majority organizations creates very stressful conditions for the newcomers, but once they are in, they generally proceed to the adjusting phase. However, because of a very prescribed and unreceptive organizational culture, the teachers in our study expressed frustrations and spoke about the need to develop meaningful coping mechanisms in order to remain productive participants in their schools. In many ways, the organizational conditions within the school impeded the ability of these teachers to progress through the same developmental process as the "successful" managers in the Dickens and Dickens (1991) study.

Fighting Discrepant Stereotypes and Qualities

Kanter's (1977) last performance pressure indicates that as a result of automatic notice and the problems of symbolic consequences, people of color in the workplace are often not recognized for their achievements. In contrast to symbolic consequences, the teachers in this study believed that they had to prove that they were "qualified." Cose (1993) contends that African Americans often have to justify their skills and abilities in order to remain in majority organizations. In this study there were differences between the male and female African American teachers in how they responded to these discrepant stereotypes. In particular, the African American males conveyed their need to make their accomplishments known because they were often fighting the "African American male stereotype," while the females felt they had to prove they were "qualified" teachers.

The male participants said that they constantly had to fight the pervasive but false stereotype that they were lazy, unreliable, irresponsible, and not intellectually driven. For them, it was not that they were recognized for their accomplishments but that they had to dispel their colleagues' misperceptions about African American males. These male teachers differed from Kanter's (1977) participants and the African American females in that they promoted their accomplishments as teachers. While they seemed uncomfortable advancing themselves with their European American colleagues, in their self-promotions their demeanor had to be casual and confident.

During their interactions with their colleagues, the African American males gave the impression that they were just as intellectual as, and the social equals of, their counterparts. Thus, in maintaining their relationships with their peers, they felt they were able to dispel the misperception of the African American male, to prove their worth to the organization, and to do acts that went beyond what their colleagues did. While they were ambivalent about promoting their work, they felt an obligation to not represent "African American male" stereotypes. The stress of performance pressures for these African American males meant they had to manage the conflicting demands placed on them by their color and social meaning at the school. A significant quote from a participant framed how he rationalized why he always had to dispel these stereotypes:

> If you're a Black teacher, if you are competent in any way, if you
> make the grade, there is the perception that the white teachers
> have about you. Some of my [European American] colleagues
> think that I can get away with a lot and be excused because I am
> Black. If you don't speak English quite so well, but you're Black,
> you'll do. It's good enough to stay here because we are filling this
> program with you. It's despicable, but it's there. You're kind of
> Teflon coated against certain things because you are Black. Like,
> they wouldn't fire me because I'm Black and they need Blacks.

Anderson (1999) states that often "within group" conflicts can result in some minority persons making another minority person feel as if he or she has sold out or has been coopted by the system. Only one of the African American male participants mentioned concerns about teaching with other African Americans at his school. He stated that he did not care if he was perceived as an "Uncle Tom" by the other African American teachers. That is, other African Americans might perceive this teacher as exceedingly loyal to the interests of the European American teachers and students, and not as a strong enough advocate for students of color. Due to performance pressures, this participant felt the need to distance himself from other African Americans in order to present himself as one who had made it despite all the odds. He believed he needed to appear open to his European American colleagues and not appear ambiguous in his social and professional relationships with other African Americans. He felt the tension that he needed to be seen as someone who was fair in his relationships with both European American teachers and children of color despite how other African American teachers might feel:

> I am going to be perceived as hard simply because I hold the
> standard true. That's not one of the easiest things to say as a
> minority teacher in a predominantly white institution. Your
> [African American] peers see you as somehow being too hard.
> Then the white teachers say, "Well, I don't want that said about
> me." But that standard is held true for white students. It's the
> same reaction from those who say I'm a sellout or an Uncle Tom
> or whatever. I really couldn't care less. It's not my problem. As
> long as I am seen as treating the kids fairly, Black or white, as
> long I am in an institution contracted to provide service with

competency and integrity, then I am offering above and beyond what I see as necessary.

The female teachers reported that they had to establish themselves as "qualified" teachers, thus overshadowing their "token" status. Though they were not fighting male stereotypes, they encountered European American teachers who believed they were affirmative-action hires. The African American teachers reported that their colleagues made them feel as though they were defined by their color. Thus, there was this underlying assumption by their European American peers that they were not "qualified" teachers. Furthermore, they felt their European American counterparts resented them because these African American teachers questioned their power and authority. Thus, as a response to their colleagues' bitterness, they felt they needed to diminish their successes as teachers:

> I thought, "I am going into a staff of teachers where they know I'm being hired because I am Black and that special concessions were being made." And I really did not want my peers looking down on me or thinking negatively. Then having to put up with the crap that goes with your peers putting you down. I just don't trust these people, so I am always wondering. Yet, when they have a difficult Black child or a problem with a Black parent, I become the person they come to.

The female teachers, unlike the males, reported that if both their African American and European American students performed well on tests or projects, their European American colleagues often sabotaged their efforts. One female African American teacher reported that her reputation for teaching difficult students became known to the school's parents. Consequently, the principal informed her that many parents requested her because of her success with students who had reading problems. Because she was recognized for her accomplishments with the more challenging learners, she encountered situations where European American teachers pulled students from her room when their academic performance improved.

The African American female teachers who taught in elementary schools believed that their presence and significant student achievements caused additional problems for them. These teachers all stated that their European American colleagues were not culturally responsive to the "deseg" children. As a result, these teachers believed there was an unwritten expectation that African American students were not to be favored or given a different set of behavioral expectations. If an African American teacher did not adhere to philosophical beliefs about standards of behavior similar to those of her European American peers, she encountered additional consequences. Thus, these teachers believed that when African American students were disciplined by European American teachers, it was in response to the African American teachers making more allowances for these students' behavior.

Only the female elementary school participants expressed concern that their principals were very naive in handling racial tensions at their school. They aired their opinions on how their principals needed to validate their teaching ability and "ready" the school for the possible negative reactions to hiring a teacher of color. The African American elementary teachers noted the shock and dismay of parents when their European American children were placed in their rooms. This resulted in some parents asking for transfers. Thus a stir was created in the school, with implications that the African American teachers were unqualified. Principals were negligent in supporting teachers of color when parents questioned their abilities. Unfortunately, negative responses to African American teachers' very presence often overshadowed their competence as teachers.

As noted earlier, it was apparent that most of the frustrations that these participants encountered were in part due to their visibility. So many of their actions were under constant scrutiny by peers, students, parents, and school leaders. In many ways they remained in what Dickens and Dickens (1991) define as the entry and adjusting phases. They continually had to be vocal in their interactions with the European American teachers, and were thus perceived as militant or uncooperative. These teachers were rarely acknowledged for their work efforts and experienced little professional growth. Eventually the African American teachers realized that they needed to move forward and focus on their successes with their students and parents.

Cultural Switching

According to the research on ethnic identity development, code switching occurs when an organization or group indicates signs of discomfort with explicit expressions of difference, especially in race matters. In such situations, African Americans act, think, dress, and express themselves in ways that maximize the comfort level of the group or organization in order to minimize their differences (Cross et al., 1999). Orbe (1998) believes that muted group communication offers insights into how the organization influences daily interactions between minority and majority groups, and that communication in dominant organizations creates an evaluative language that is used to create group solidarity and oppression. These communication strategies create a "mutedness" in which people of color are hesitant to address inequities and have developed their own communication patterns.

In addition to Kanter's (1977) performance pressures, our interviews revealed a new theme, *cultural switching* (Madsen & Mabokela, 2000). In our research, we identified cultural switching, a process similar to code switching, in which our participants employed strategies to negotiate the cultural dissonance between themselves and the culture of their schools and their European American colleagues. Analysis of the male data did not reveal that those participants attempted cultural switching strategies as a coping mechanism. Based on the findings, we cannot conclude that male teachers were better at handling performance pressures; they simply employed different strategies.

Our analysis revealed that the female teachers expressed more dissonance between their cultural norms and values and those of their European American colleagues. This may in part be due to responding to performance pressures and confronting power relationships within the organization. The incongruence between the norms and values of these two groups of teachers necessitated cultural switching, a process through which African American teachers adjusted to and negotiated the norms of their European American school culture. There were very few teachers of color in these schools, a factor that prevented them from developing a "kinship" to assist them with their acculturation. African American teachers cited strategies that they soon developed upon entering their schools, many of them emerging through trial-and-error processes.

Upon entering their suburban desegregated schools, the female African American teachers experienced cultural incongruence in their knowing, understanding, and expression of their ideas about teaching with European American colleagues. All of them found themselves constrained and unable to use their social cues to navigate their schools' institutional culture. Each participant described frustrations in understanding and embracing the cultural norms and values of her school. Analysis of the data indicated two distinct processes for how these participants developed strategies for interacting with European American teachers. Some of the female teachers learned normative cues by being diplomatic learners who spent their time observing and testing their perceptions about their interactions with their colleagues. The other method was characterized as being direct, forthright, and assertive. As the African American teachers maneuvered through this process of cultural switching, they were better equipped to protect themselves and to address prejudices they encountered.

Many of the female teachers expressed the need to be diplomatic learners and experimented slowly in asserting themselves in productive ways. Participants who adopted diplomatic strategies in their cultural switching were concerned with how they were perceived by the European American faculty and how they interacted with them socially and professionally. Their intent was to dispel stereotypical myths that often pervaded their conversations with these teachers. Over time, they became adept at asserting themselves without appearing "militant." These participants believed that keeping a low profile was important for their transition at the school. After an extended period, they developed more one-on-one relationships with some European American teachers, but they were still cautious in their interactions:

> Assimilation in the workplace is just another place where African Americans have to assimilate in order to play the game, to get where you want to go, or to fit in. If I were an African American in the school and I was Black Power, and I said, "Let's hold a rally," or "Let's do a march," or "Why are you looking at me because I'm two minutes late? Is it because I am Black?" how

long would I be here? So you can't wear your anger and your mission on your shoulders. There is a way to make change and help white people become more aware of things. But a riotous attitude or being aggressive doesn't work here. I learned by watching the faculty how to get your ideas across or help people to try to understand things better.

Those teachers who used a more diplomatic process stated that they developed strategies to make their points known without intimidating the European American faculty. Some participants stated that they acquired cultivated responses to race-related questions. They also learned how to develop a body language that would not reveal their uneasiness in their interactions with European American faculty. Usually within the first 2 years, they began to voice their opinions, knowing that the European American faculty would be more amenable to their suggestions.

In sharp contrast, the other female teachers used a more assertive approach in their cultural switching and were more outspoken in their views. They challenged what they perceived as unfair and racist treatment of students. Some of the participants felt that being direct and speaking out in their interactions with European American faculty was essential to asserting themselves. By affirming their presence, they pushed their own beliefs and values. These strong individuals would not allow their colleagues to take advantage of them or to repress their sense of self. They interpreted their colleagues' cultural norms as racist, so they assumed a combative role. Two participants talked about how they told European American faculty members to change what they perceived as prejudicial practices or tendencies when teaching African American students. For these participants, making "your voice known" was important to ensure that their colleagues could not still their voices. Once their presence was established, they relaxed their guard, but their suspicions about European Americans were always in the forefront.

Conclusion

In this chapter we discussed the findings from a case study that examined how intergroup differences created performance pressures for African American teachers and how this affected their ability to contribute optimally in desegregated suburban school environments. Our findings, based on the experiences of 14 self-reported accounts of African American teachers in these school environments, illuminated patterns of experiences for teachers of color. While we do not claim to generalize broadly to other suburban desegregated contexts, the experiences articulated by the African American teachers do help us understand the complexities of intergroup differences.

The participants in our study developed a variety of responses to the pressures they experienced in their suburban school environments. In response to *automatic notice*, our first theme, teachers developed strategies that assisted them in their transitions to inhospitable environments in the suburban schools. The female teachers reported the need for a strong reference group orientation that would enable them to retain their cultural identity within the school. While the female teachers viewed automatic notice negatively, the male participants recognized their high visibility as a way to compete against their peers. That is, in environments where there are few teachers of color, there is a certain cultural dissonance that results in African American teachers having to protect themselves from unfair scrutiny by other school participants (teachers, students, and parents).

Dealing with *symbolic consequences*, the second emergent theme, underrepresented individuals often bear the burden of dispelling myths and representing their race in their exchanges with coworkers. It was apparent that the European American teachers had had minimal exposure to others who were different from them because their cultural identity was based on what Cox (1993) calls a monocultural identity. Therefore, the African American participants in our study were continually under pressure to refute stereotypical comments that European American teachers expressed to them. In addition, these teachers were placed in situations where they would have to negotiate their racial associations with the European American teachers. If they appeared "too white" or "too Black" in their professional exchanges with these teachers, they were concerned that this might compromise their own cultural identity and associations with other African American teachers at the school. The African American teachers also became resistant to representing their race. In many ways, they expressed the notion that their European American colleagues expected them to take ownership of issues that affected only the African American children. These teachers were compromised by this narrow definition of their expertise and disliked their limited role as the "minority representative."

In fighting *discrepant stereotypes*, the third theme, the underrepresented African American teachers had to defend their status in order to have their accomplishments recognized. They reported that their individuality was often overshadowed by their colleagues' stereotypical beliefs about African Americans. The male teachers constantly had to refute the negative "African American male stereotype," while the women had to deal with proving their worth as "qualified" teachers. As a way of coping with these prejudices and the low expectations from their European American colleagues, these participants experienced an internalized pressure to outperform their counterparts, yet were never recognized for their accomplishments except in their role as the "Black expert."

The final pressure, what we call *cultural switching*, became apparent as the African American female teachers expressed the heaviness of being in an environment where they were often one of a few or the only person of color in the school. They struggled with the cultural incongruency between them and their European American peers. In many ways these performance pressures resulted in their feeling constrained and unable to use social cues to navigate their school's culture. In learning to culture switch, these teachers developed coping strategies of being either direct or diplomatic observers in learning to find their place in these contexts.

Our findings indicate the prevalence of a strong organizational culture within desegregated suburban schools that created performance pressures for African American teachers. As a result of the incongruence between the culture of the school and the norms and values of the teachers of color, this counterculture prevented the development of a shared intergroup culture.

As a result of our findings, an important question remains: How do European American schools develop an organizational culture that supports teachers of color? It is apparent that strategies are needed to create a more positive social context for minority teachers in which European American teachers are in the majority. When minority teachers are hired, there is an expectation that these individuals will serve as the "Black experts" and provide that context for the school. European American colleagues fail to understand the differences that exist within minority cultures, and instead project narrowly defined roles for these African American teachers. Much like the interviewees in Dickens and Dickens (1991), these teachers struggled with their entry phase in these contexts. These teachers experienced a range of emotions that may have affected their adjustment phase. Teachers often struggled with how to fit in and were limited in how they could interact with their peers.

African American teachers in this study believed they were prevented from contributing to the school because their function was conceived as, and restricted to, representing the "Black perspective." The dominant culture's stereotypical views and beliefs about teachers further restrained the effectiveness of African American teachers. To protect a school's espoused beliefs about the views of a minority group, the district was apt to hire African Americans who were perceived as "safe" and less likely to challenge the school's perceptions about African American students and teachers. This tendency may lead teachers of color to feel that they must lose their cultural identity if they are hired in these contexts.

2
Intergroup Differences and Group Boundaries: Implications for Inclusive Schools

Introduction

This chapter examines cultural differences between the teachers of color and the European American teachers, which create group boundaries and intergroup differences. Due to these group boundaries, there is the expectation by the majority school participants that the African American teachers will conform to dominant practices and embrace the norms, values, and culture of the organization. Because there are so few African American teachers in these contexts, these teachers experienced boundary heightening; that is, the heightened awareness of differences that exist between majority and minority group members in a given work environment (Cox, 1994). In our study, boundary heightening became apparent for both the male and the female participants in their interactions with their colleagues around issues of (1) pedagogical differences and management strategies, (2) dispelling negative stereotypes that European American teachers held about children of color, and (3) negotiating their insider-outsider status with European American colleagues.

Intergroup Differences and Boundary Heightening

Cox (1994) contends that cultural identity adds another layer of complexity in how people are socialized and incorporated into the organization. "Cultural" identity addresses our sense of ourselves as cultural beings; that identity comes to be reflected in the norms and values that characterize our feelings as members of our cultural group (or groups). Cox (1994) further argues that variations among norms and values held by different groups (cultural identity group and organizational group) result in intergroup tensions within the workplace, tensions evident in the phenomenon that the degree of distinction workers are likely to attain in their careers is inversely proportional to their degree of physical distinctiveness.

The significance of intergroup theory for understanding individual identity helps to conceptualize the effects of diverse identities within a larger organizational context (Nkomo & Cox, 1996). Key issues of intergroup theory related to issues of diversity include (1) the circumstances that lead to the formation of groups, their boundaries, roles, and development cycle; (2) the effects of population membership, group membership, and intergroup dynamics in dealing with prejudices; and (3) the problems of identity, power, conflict, and social comparisons in groups (Watts, 1994). Several studies reflect what occurs when a person from another group who is different from the majority enters the organization (Anderson, 1999; Cose, 1993; Kanter, 1977). It is apparent from these studies that differences within and between identity and organizational groups create sources of intergroup conflict resulting in unequal power groups with poor relations among the different groups, and determine how roles are structured within the groups.

Having a cultural identity different from that of the majority in an organization can impact every aspect of the career experience for people of color (Cox, 1994). People of color are continually pressured to enact behaviors that may not be natural for them, making them have to become, in a sense, two different people. Individuals can feel that they have to sacrifice their identity in order to retain their job. Minority group members experience conflict over how to react and refrain from critiquing day-to-day decisions. This conflict is complicated by the fact that majority workers are often ignorant about other cultures and insensitive to cultural tensions in the workplace. Thus, they misinterpret the behavior of persons of color, especially when they are silent, or they criticize them for the way they assume roles and responsibilities. As a result of diverse identities in the workplace, a majority group solidarity is created so that people of color feel the pressure to conform (Cox, 1994).

Kanter (1977) argues that the presence of minority workers causes majority workers to create a boundary heightening. This results in a polarization in which the majority group views the person of color as an outsider and expects him or her to conform to the organization's norms and socialization process. Majority workers create group solidarity by emphasizing those cultural elements (norms, role specialization, boundaries, etc.) that they share in contrast to the minority person. Consequently, what often occurs is a validation process of majority group solidarity, and the camaraderie, telling of racial jokes, and undermining become sanctioned by the majority group. A consistent testing to reinforce the norms of the group is established (Kanter, 1976).

Another aspect of boundary heightening results in ensuring that the person of color is made to feel like an outsider. An in-group understanding forms, which results in minority workers feeling like outsiders through subtle reminders that there are differences among them. These "reminders of difference" force minorities into preexisting generalizations, which results in their being role entrapped within the organization. As a result of role entrapment, minorities have to cope with status leveling and stereotyped role induction.

Boundary heightening often results in overt inhibition, so that majority workers engage in certain activities that would not necessarily be done in the company of minority workers (Kanter, 1976). As a result, minorities in the workplace become isolated and are not privy to the inner workings of the organization. People of color are then given closer scrutiny in which majority workers discuss their job performance and ways to get around company policies, and develop strategies to prevent minority workers from advancing within the organization.

When they are made to feel like outsiders and are left out of majority networks, people of color often feel forced to accept the culture of the majority. Because there are so few people of color in these contexts, there is no opportunity to establish a counterculture or to develop an intergroup network (Kanter, 1977; Morrison, 1996). Consequently, minorities have two choices: they can accept the isolation that results from their being excluded or they can create a "polarization" in which they separate themselves from other minorities as a way of fitting the majority's expectations. This environment provides a compelling example of the type of structure that does not allow for differences.

Results of Boundary Heightening

Our research indicates that boundary heightening was very apparent for the African American teachers we interviewed. Because of their high visibility, there was the expectation that they should conform to the traditional practices that the European American teachers used. When these teachers entered these contexts, they were often the only one or one of a few, so in many ways there were perceived as outsiders. Hence, according to Kanter (1977), European American teachers felt comfortable making racist comments in their presence. The European American teachers created such a strong group solidarity that many of the African American teachers remained silent in order to retain their own sense of identity. While many of the African American teachers were recognized for their ability to improve outcomes for both European American students and students of color, they were often trapped in their roles as the "Black expert" during faculty meetings.

The following portion of this chapter provides insights into the intergroup differences that created tensions between the African American teachers and the European American school participants. The boundary heightening could be seen in the way the European American teachers created a group solidarity through (1) their assumption that the minority teachers should use traditional management and instructional practices, (2) their insensitivity in making negative comments, and (3) the implications for their insider-outsider role.

Pedagogical Mismatch and Management Differences

Because the African American teachers perceived the institutional culture of their schools as not supportive of their use of culturally relevant instructional practices, boundaries became evident in their relationships with the European American teachers. The participants in this study noted the cultural differences related to the instructional practices of their European American peers. Many of the African American teachers noted tension in their relationships with European American peers when they perceived the pedagogical practices of their colleagues as nonresponsive to children of color. Many of the participants noted differences between their instructional and management practices and those of their colleagues. However, the male African American teachers were more vocal about instructional differences, while the female African American teachers felt that their colleagues were unfair in their management practices.

Cox (1994) states that in majority organizations, when there are dissimilarities between groups, a culturally based hesitancy evolves in regard to making these differences apparent. While these African American teachers were aware of differences between them and their peers in their instructional practices, they became silent rather than speaking out or being critical of their peers. Interestingly enough, neither the veteran nor the less experienced African American participants approached their colleagues about their instructional practices. They thought that by creating boundaries around pedagogical differences, they created more problems for themselves and the students of color.

Two of the male participants stated that their school was based on a European American tradition in which traditional instructional practices prevailed. Additional studies, such as Scofield (1989) and Wells and Crain (1997), have noted that teachers in suburban districts (with desegregated schools) similar to this district used "color-blind" pedagogical practices in which teachers taught children of color in the same way as the other children. Therefore, this "color-blind" perspective resulted in teachers' limited understanding of using culturally relevant pedagogical practices. One male participant noted:

> There are some theoretical underpinnings in the way schools are structured. They are essentially structured for the middle-class

European American child. A Black child interacting in a traditional setting like my district may need more from that teacher simply because assumptions are made about what the teaching style will be or the learning style of the student, and so forth. It is not geared toward that minority kid. Their experiences are not taken into account in relation to the experiences that the average European American child has when they interact in the same classroom.

The male teachers also believed that many students of color failed in these suburban schools through their colleagues' unwillingness to modify their pedagogical practices. Two male participants also reported that European American teachers had different academic expectations for students of color. While many male participants commented about their European American colleagues' practices, they were hesitant to address these issues with their colleagues. Because of the boundary heightening that occurred at the school, many of the participants were often silent on how students of color were taught:

People say things that are offensive, and I know a lot of teachers that I run into, they don't know how Blacks communicate, and they think a fight is going on, and they're just being loud. Sometimes they [European American teachers] use strict discipline, and you gotta have a little flexibility, especially for our Black students. You have to be somewhat flexible until there's some trust built up. For some of the students, it's like going into the Marine Corps. It's a culture shock. And as much a shock for the students as it is for the teachers.

At the elementary level the female African American teachers noted that their differences with their colleagues were in the area of discipline. These participants felt that European American teachers believed in the use of power and control in employing traditional management practices. These female teachers reported that using these practices was problematic because they created more problems for the African American students. In comparison, the African American teachers at the elementary level stated that they employed a flexible management style and developed more one-on-one strategies for their students. These female teachers noted that they felt they were criticized by their

European American colleagues for not being harder on the "deseg" children at the school.

Negative Stereotypes

Both the elementary and secondary African American teachers reported that their European American colleagues held negative beliefs about African American children. They concluded that their colleagues gained information about students of color through other European American teachers, resulting in the promotion of stereotypes. As a result, these participants reported that the European American teachers held low expectations for the "deseg" students, used unfair grading practices, and placed African American students in low-achieving classes. African American teachers reported that their counterparts' negative stereotypes resulted in attributional information that was subtly conveyed to African American children. All participants stated that their focus was always on the child, and they noted that the European American teachers were hesitant to change their perceptions about students of color. One teacher reported:

> The grading practices of white teachers are so subtle. Some of it has to do with position and power. I deeply believe white teachers give themselves the privilege of giving African American kids lower grades, because their experience has been that the parent may not fight as hard. And their head set is that they are not as bright as the other kids. Black children here are adult shy and do not know how to brownnose like the white children do. It makes a difference. When I looked at the remedial grouping, I saw they were all Black children. That's when I clearly saw color and how white teachers here place students. I had a hard time understanding why. Why are Black kids always the ones that are low? I then work with these children so they are successful; even the white children improve. It just goes to show you how biased these teachers are.

Insider-Outsider Role

As noted in Kanter's (1977) research, the African American teachers in this study occupied a dual "insider-outsider" status within their work environment. On the one hand, they were seen as "insiders" who provided insights about students of color and shared their expertise about African American-related issues. On the other hand, they were treated as "outsiders" whose narrowly defined "Black expertise" resulted in their being isolated and unable to attain any informal social power. Most of the participants accepted their function as the resident "Black expert" but often were troubled by how their insider role was perceived by European American teachers and other African American teachers. The male and female African American teachers perceived their insider-outsider role differently.

The male participants willingly embraced their insider role as a way to edify and sensitize their European American colleagues about African American students. While they perceived themselves as the communication links for school participants, they often said they did not feel comfortable in their associations with colleagues. They noted the discomfort of assuming leadership on only African American concerns, yet they felt their opinions were highly valued. The male teachers noted that addressing only multicultural issues limited their ability to share with colleagues on other educational matters. While they willingly accepted the insider role and were willing to spend time with their European American colleagues discussing issues related to African American students, they felt the boundaries of being treated like the outsider. As outsiders, the male participants sensed tension between them and their European American counterparts, especially on issues relating to the educational needs of African American students and their parents:

> If they are hiring, it would be valuable to hire Black teachers for the white children in this district. That would be first and foremost. Hire Black teachers so that the white children in this district could have a positive experience with Black people. They should be hiring white teachers who have the capacity to establish positive relationships with Black children. They are letting [white] teachers off the hook by not expecting them to have positive relationships with the minority kids. They just dump them on some Black teachers that they hire. We need you [white teachers] to help carry this weight. As a Black teacher, I have a responsibility to every child who comes into my room. I can't be

the teacher for the Black children mainly. It does not work out that way.

The female teachers experienced similar reminders that the only reason they were hired was their skin color, and felt this impacted how they were regarded at the school. Thus, they became recognized as the "Black experts" and were made to feel they were hired to teach only the African American students. The female African American teachers, in contrast to the males, often were unhappy and felt they were being used, and did not welcome opportunities to address "insider" roles because they were constant reminders that they were "outsiders." The female participants felt that the European American teachers failed to acknowledge differences that existed among members of one minority group. For example, the African American teachers discussed their interactions with African American students and the difficulties they experienced in gaining the trust of some students. This was particularly true for those African American students who perceived the African American teachers as "sellouts." It was apparent that the European American faculty members were unaware of these trust issues and expected the African American teachers would be responsible for all African American students, as this statement from a female teacher illustrates:

> These teachers here think I know everything about Black children, but I never grew up in the city and have never experienced the difficulties these students have had. I have to gain the trust of these students because sometimes they think I am not an advocate for them. I have to go out of my way with some students to identify with them. Yet, the teachers expect me to have success with every Black student, and I find that really troubling.

The African American female teachers also noted that their role as the resident "Black expert" absolved European American teachers from being culturally responsive to African American students. Several of the female participants noted that when student placements were made, many African American students were placed in their rooms. Furthermore, European American teachers believed that unmanageable European American children would also benefit from having an

African American teacher. While these African American teachers stated "they were there for the students," they grew weary of complete ownership of minority causes. As one of them noted:

> We were placing kids and we were trying to get a group. We didn't really know what kids would be best. And so when the teacher took the list down to the chief [the principal], he goes, "Well, just put all the Black ones in her room. Black folks like other Black folks." So this is the type of logic that I have to deal with. He's a Black problem child; put him in her room. Black teachers are supposed to be disciplinarians. "Put him in there, she can deal with it." It's just a lot of ignorance. I had a higher number of Black students in my room. I'd have four or five and everybody else would have one or two. After I was there a while, I said to the principal, "Spread this out. If we are gonna give them a nice experience here, then they shouldn't all be with me, should they?" A change was made right away, but only because I requested it.

As the minority spokespersons, the female teachers stated that they spent their time explaining to European Americans why "Black folk do what they do." Questions of why African American children do not make eye contact, why they always sit together, and why they wear their hair in a certain manner were continually presented to them. They often felt their role was to respond to European American teachers' questions about African American students. While they found their role as the "Black experts" meaningful, it also had its disadvantages. Because there were so few teachers of color at the school, being identified as "Black experts" became a risk for them. The African American teachers believed their colleagues were consumed with the idea that they should assume this role at the school.

> Part of the problem we are facing here at the school is that these teachers have no knowledge of their [Black students'] culture. And they [European American teachers] expected them to be like the majority culture. They wouldn't accept any slang talk at all. Even in children's private conversations, teachers have told them not to talk like that. It's a different language, and they need to use it.

Conclusion

As a result of boundary heightening in these suburban desegregated contexts, African American teachers dealt with a majority group of teachers who negatively reinforced the cultural differences. In many ways the European American teachers subtly reminded these teachers that they were "outsiders" who would never be fully included in their schools. In other ways, the African American teachers were perceived as "insiders" who provided information on issues of diversity, but were treated as "outsiders" who were never seen out of their race. They were recognized as outstanding teachers, yet their peers saw them only as "Black experts."

In schools wishing to create inclusive environments that attract and retain a diverse group of teachers, several things must be considered to reduce boundary heightening. To lessen intergroup tensions in these contexts, there must be frequent conversations about instructional practices and discipline issues. Teachers of color and majority teachers must be willing to address their differences. Bell (2002) believes that open communication practices are important. The inclusion of all voices within the organization provides a clear understanding for establishing a level playing field. Teachers of color can reduce intergroup conflict by being translators for both European American teachers and students of color (Bell, 2002).

The expectation that teachers of color will play an "insider" versus an "outsider" role can be structurally eliminated. Organizational structures (teaming, mentoring, and technical support) often prevent teachers from participating in school issues. Organizational goals should focus on the individual talents of these teachers so that the focus is not on hiring them only as the "Black expert." Schools need to ensure participatory structures that support team structures and to encourage an organizational socialization that supports the addressing of cultural differences. Additionally, as Dickens and Dickens (1991) state, as people of color enter into majority organizations, they go through the entry and adjusting phase. Teachers of color must be supported in order to prevent "protective hesitation," so they will not feel the need to isolate themselves and withdraw from colleagues.

There are a number of strategies to ensure an inclusive school when attracting and retaining teachers of color. One method is to educate the existing teachers about cultural differences and behavioral concerns. Again, dialogue about differences is a good thing if it is well managed and there is a concerted effort to ensure that all voices are heard. Another option is to hire and promote those teachers who are open, tolerant, and flexible on matters of diversity. These individuals will support diversity change initiatives within the school. Teachers who are more tolerant and accepting of group differences will produce less intergroup conflict. Negative responses to cultural differences are sometimes nothing more than emotional or affective responses to others who are different. Structured interactions within the school are vital to eliminating intergroup differences. Departmental meetings should focus on understanding cultural differences and what they mean for students and teachers of color in creating an inclusive school.

3
ROLE ENTRAPMENT AND THE GLASS CEILING

Introduction

Our findings reveal that African American teachers in suburban schools tend to be entrapped in particular roles, a practice that has limited their ability to utilize their full range of talents and expertise. In this chapter we explore ways in which the teachers in our study became entrapped and how they negotiated this limiting behavior to become meaningfully engaged in their school environments. The teachers in our study expressed concerns about being entrapped in particular roles within their school. That is, their expertise was defined to fit preexisting generalizations that forced them into playing limited roles within the organization (Kanter, 1977). Thus, they became trapped as the "token," a position that invalidated their other contributions within the school and limited their upward mobility to positions of authority. Due to role entrapment, there is a tendency for majority group members to have stereotypical assumptions and to fit "tokens" into preexisting generalizations. In these areas, the male and female African American teachers in our study reacted differently in how they perceived their districts' practice of entrapment.

Role Entrapment and the Glass Ceiling

Some studies have attempted to address the intersection of race and gender that defines the cultural ideological context in which these factors affect workplace relationships (Ransford & Miller, 1983). There is ample evidence that women and people of color are disadvantaged in finding their way into organizations and are disproportionately found in lower-level occupations with less chance for individual promotion (Miller, Labovitz, & Fry, 1975). Little research has dealt directly with the experiences of people of color in organizations, but it can be argued that patterns of race relations may be similar to those of gender (Miller, Lincoln, & Olson, 1981). Butler's (1976) research states that, independent of ability and training, race factors are found to have a direct effect on being promoted. Racial dynamics in the organization also leads to limited numbers of people of color being promoted to higher levels.

Kanter's (1977) study of women in the workplace and Cose's (1993) study of the "dozen demons" that often plague people of color in the workplace have implications for how minorities are perceived and treated in the workplace. Their research indicates that often there is a belief that certain tasks or expertise is best handled by a person of color; consequently, the person of color is trapped in certain roles. Such a belief system in organizations results in pigeonholing people of color. They are acknowledged only on the basis of their skin color; thus they become role entrapped and never promoted within the organization.

Kanter (1977) defines multiple aspects of role entrapment that demonstrate that people of color experience "status leveling." Status leveling occurs when members of the majority group within the organization assume, when they encounter a person of color, that that person has a menial job in the organization. Often women's and people of color's workplace status is assumed by their coworkers to be lower than that of the positions they actually occupy, and it is a struggle for them to establish accurate and appropriate role relations to ensure their position, if indeed they ever manage to. Stopping the practice of status leveling involves adjusting the majority workers' perceptions, so people of color can be seen in their appropriate employment standing (Kanter, 1977).

Another aspect of role entrapment is "stereotyped role induction." When people of color enter the organization, the majority tends to hold stereotypical beliefs about certain groups. If people of color do not fit these preconceived societal expectations, such as speaking or acting a certain way, then they have to continually validate their place within the organization (Kanter, 1977). This logic implies certain self-fulfilling assumptions about race that result in the hiring people of color only for certain entry-level positions within the organization. People of color become encapsulated, expected to match the stereotypes the majority holds about their minority group (Kanter, 1977).

Morrison (1996) writes about the glass ceiling and its implications for recruitment and retention of women and people of color. There are multiple barriers that restrict the opportunities and rewards available to these groups. The most important of these barriers has implications for teachers of color in majority schools. These obstacles have to do with prejudice in treating differences as weaknesses, a lonely and unsupportive working environment, and the natural tendency for districts to hire people like the majority (Morrison, 1996). Schools have struggled with minority recruitment issues for a long time. One challenge in recruiting teachers of color in majority contexts has been the problem of establishing a collective identity. Thus, in majority schools, teachers of color are often isolated rather than embedded in relationships with other teachers when the schools lack an inclusive culture (Gordon, 2000).

While districts state that they are hiring teachers of color for their schools, they often establish subjective criteria that result in differential treatment for teachers of color. Afraid that persons of color might fail in a higher-status job, management often delays promotion for these individuals. Morrison (1996) believes that cultural differences are problematic because they perpetuate the belief that it is easier to relate to someone with the same values, the same looks, and the same perceptions. Therefore, discomfort with someone who is ethnically different and the use of higher standards to evaluate people of color results in problems with their being hired and promoted.

Role Entrapment and Its Implications for Teachers of Color

In the ensuing discussion we examine how the African American teachers we interviewed became trapped in these school contexts. In many ways these teachers of color felt that they were hired to support the desegregation policies. Often, they struggled with their place and felt they were perceived as affirmative action hires. In addition, many of them struggled with how to respond to their peers once they were hired. How could these teachers of color ensure their place and be accepted as added value? Dreaming further, how could their contributions be seen as a cultural asset whereby they could bring their background, socialization, and experiences to solve learning issues for all students? To get back to reality, though, they became nothing more than "Black experts" thanks to the misperceptions of the majority teachers.

The male African American teachers reported that the only reason they were hired was to support the desegregation policies and to attain a racial balance in the suburban districts. They viewed entrapment as low status and low expectations of them. These males also stated that the district was unable to hire teachers of color because of its assumption that African Americans must conform to the district's organizational culture. These teachers noted that the district's rationale for hiring them was to represent the African American perspective and provide the school participants with their expertise on African American students. They also believed that this role entrapment was problematic in how districts hired other teachers of color. The male participants noted the issue of trust with their school colleagues and always having to wonder if they were going beyond the stereotypical views that European Americans held about teachers of color:

> It is interesting to look and listen to different people. I remember years ago I was talking to a teacher who said he was from a small town. He was saying that students were given vacation at the harvest period. He said, "You know about that." I said, "I am sorry, I really don't know anything about that." I am Black, and I should know about picking cotton and working as a migrant laborer. Other times people said, "You served in Switzerland, Canada, and France. Did you get a scholarship?" I said "no." They wanted to figure out how I got there.

Several of the male participants noted that there was an expectation that they should be more European American in dress, language, and interests. As a result of this perspective, African American teachers would not want to completely mold themselves to this monocultural environment. Many of the male teachers noted that the reason their district struggled to find "qualified" teachers of color was that prospective African American teachers would lose their sense of who they were by being there. The district's expectation to hire teachers who were like-minded and similar-looking also meant that African American teachers were expected to use the same traditional methods as their peers. Many of the participants believed that the district's recruitment efforts to hire African American teachers only for their expertise led to their becoming role trapped. This affected the district's efforts to recruit additional African American teachers. The following statement represents how most of the male participants felt about their district's lack of recruitment efforts:

> I think there are very good reasons why [other African American teachers] don't want to come out to the suburbs. For many it would be a hassle. First they have to disrupt their social life where they have to make new friends and they have to be more perfect and please people and cut across cultural lines. That can be a hassle. You've got to socialize on their terms. It was a hassle particularly to me. People get tired of proving themselves. They don't want to go through the negatives that exist with parents and the children. They might not get support from administration. You can't trust them. You might be lucky and get someone who is a positive support. So teaching in the suburbs is not just roses, honey, and cream.

The female participants also commented that their districts were looking for African American teachers who were similar to the European American teachers. Three of the female teachers who had been with the district the longest thought the district hired "white-looking" African American teachers. In the early days, when districts were responding to hiring quotas, there was a progression to hiring fair-skinned minorities. One of the female veteran African Americans believed that at first the district hired very "white-looking" African American female teachers, then eventually moved to darker-skinned African American women. She observed:

> The teachers started coming in. I did notice the district tended to hire ... light-skinned Black people. I guess they sort of edged them in. I don't consider myself one, but maybe I don't look .... Maybe I look a little Hispanic. I'm not sure what they thought .... But anyway they didn't hire any dark-skinned Black teachers until a while passed and then they edged them in after that. I saw the progression: women first, faired-skinned, darker women, males. Seemingly that was the progression.

Some of the female participants stated that African American males were given closer scrutiny than the African American females. One of the female teachers believed that many of the European American female teachers were often uncomfortable with having a Black male at their school:

> Black males in the district are looked upon as fearful by female parents, and I think by some female teachers. It's one of those things that were really funny to see. Mr. Smith [an African American male at the school] was this tall, darker-skinned, handsome Black man, but I was surprised to hear how many white women talked openly about their feelings about him and his deep voice. Yet, when I talked to another white woman teacher, she tells me how she is so afraid when she goes to bed at night that a Black man might rape her.

The African American female teachers agreed that these districts hired "safe Blacks." Outspoken African Americans who had an agenda of addressing racial inequities at a school were either given difficult working conditions or isolated from other African American teachers. Those African Americans who understood the codes of power and the appropriate language and dress were more suited as the "token Black," as these comments reflect:

> A Black male who used to work in this district was conscious to the depths ... and very vocal. He ended up leaving because of that. At another school in this district they also had a Black male, very outspoken. I didn't see any problem [with him], but the school did.

Another participant concurred:

> There's a very small percentage of Blacks here who are outspoken. There is this hidden pressure to conform or they make life so difficult, you have to leave to save your sense of purpose.

Anderson (1999) contends that majority organizations believe the presentation of self, including minority candidates' dress and demeanor and general social outlook, is important to how effective they are within the organization. The participants in this study believed their districts perceived them as one monolithic group and were unable to treat them as individuals. Thus, they became entrapped as the "token," a position that invalidated their other contributions within the school and short-changed their upward mobility to positions of authority.

Conclusion

Role entrapment refers to the idea that in some work environments, majority group members have preexisting generalizations that they believe nonmajority group members fit and that force the nonmajority group into playing limited roles within the organization (Kanter, 1977). Therefore, the expertise and contributions of the minority group members are limited by the narrow vision of their majority colleagues. Therefore, the sartorial, postural, and facial appearance of the minority group members are potent sites for judicious dissent.

The participants in this study believed their districts perceived them as a monolithic group and were unable to treat them as individuals. In dealing with role entrapment, the male and female African American teachers reacted differently in how they perceived their districts' response in hiring teachers of color. In this study, the teachers realized that they were hired in order to support the desegregation policies and to attain racial balance in the suburban districts. Therefore, their contributions were limited by this restricted delineation of their expertise.

The burden for teachers of color to represent their demographic group while serving as "Black experts" results in role entrapment within the organization. Because teachers of color represent not only their school but also their ethnic group, they are constantly called upon to promote a diversity agenda (Morrison, 1996). Diversity being in the sorry state it is, teachers of color are under considerable pressure to do more. Teachers of color who choose not to support diversity activities run the risk of alienating both other teachers of color and majority teachers. Their visibility leaves them no refuge from multiple, sometimes conflicting, obligations. Add to these challenges that teachers of color face not being recognized for their other contributions and an absence of professional and collegial support. Perhaps this is why teachers of color often leave.

There are no easy solutions to recruiting and retaining teachers of color. Despite its widespread use, role entrapment is not a successful retention technique and wastes valuable resources. Often districts recruit without any provisions for retention strategies. But it becomes apparent that if districts are committed to recruiting teachers of color, they have to have a strategic process that specifically targets people of color. This implies that personnel directors should seek to establish partnerships or cooperative programs with diverse sources such as historically Black colleges and universities. Another practice may be to establish a "wait-and-see" period during which schools hire temporary teachers who may later become full-time employees (Morrison, 1996). Recruitment of teachers of color should involve more than just visiting teacher fairs and hoping districts will be able to hire these individuals. Research overwhelmingly suggests that progressive schools have to make major changes in their traditional recruitment strategies. They have to change their primary sources for recruits and they have to adopt different techniques in their retention practices.

PART II

LEADERSHIP CHALLENGES IN A DIVERSE WORKPLACE: UNDERSTANDING INTERGROUP DIFFERENCES TO CREATE INCLUSIVE SCHOOLS

In part II, we examine what it means to lead in diverse contexts and the considerations an administrator needs to address in working with professionals who may be racially and ethnically different from her or him. School administrators need to understand how mainstream leadership theories, in not stressing the significance of understanding cultural identity and its relationship to intergroup conflict in creating an inclusive work climate, do not serve them well in diverse environments. We have learned from our research on organizations that ignoring or

attempting to suppress cultural differences can result in negative outcomes for organizations, groups, and individuals (Madsen &
Mabokela, 2000; Mabokela & Madsen, 2003a; Ferdman, 1995).
Therefore, this part of the book will (1) provide a rationale for how
leadership and diversity are connected, (2) provide a research perspective on how school leaders perceive intergroup differences, and (3)
share additional insights on the importance of diversity self-efficacy
and its implications for creating inclusive schools.

Rationale for the Connection Between Leadership and Diversity

Increasing diversity among teachers and students is one of the most
critical adaptive challenges that leaders face in creating excellent
schools. Ethnic, racial, and many other differences (and similarities)
between school participants and administrators influence perceptions
and expectations between teachers and students. In order for any school
to achieve high levels of performance, students from all backgrounds
and demographic groups must be engaged in doing what it takes to
maximize learning opportunities and outcomes, and for a rich variety of
people this calls for a rich variety of approaches. However, despite the
goal of balanced performance across demographic groups, evidence
shows that general school performance is still disparate across ethnic
and racial lines. The job of ensuring high-quality performance by
teachers, and ultimately students, in multicultural school settings falls
on the shoulders of the school principal.

Leadership and diversity are invariably connected as schools move
from monocultural, nondiverse contexts to ones that contain ethnically
diverse, multilingual, and economically disadvantaged children. Therefore, school leaders must understand the complexity of cultural identity
structure and its implications for intergroup conflict. Cox (1994) uses the
concept of cultural identity structure to refer to an individual's particular
configuration of membership in cultural groups. Leaders need to grasp
the importance of cultural identity in order to understand how individuals view themselves in terms of their membership in identity groups and
how that impacts their organizational group membership. Thus, the cultural identity of people in organizations is a function of both their group
membership and their organizational group membership (Cox, 1994).

The concept of cultural identity is defined as a person's individual image of the cultural features that characterize his or her group(s) and the reflection of these features in his or her self-representation. The utilization of cultural identity allows us to understand systematic variations in how people see themselves as connected to their group(s) and serves to examine how diversity at the individual level affects group-level differences (Ferdman, 1995). Therefore, as we prepare leaders, they need to understand how to conceptualize cultural identities from the individual perspective and what that means in responding to group differences.

The term *diversity* has many resonances that create challenges in how it is likely to be interpreted. Care should be taken in using it, lest diversity be construed so broadly as to mean any difference between people, or so narrowly defined as to be limited only to differences of gender and race. The organizational diversity literature has been linked to leadership, but through a very narrow pathway (DiTomaso & Hooijberg, 1996). Leaders must be seen as agents of influence who understand how a person's cultural identity influences his or her organizational membership. Leaders in diverse contexts must incorporate interpersonal and intergroup interactions, organizational transformation, studies of inequality, and moral and ethical structure into their framework to address diversity issues. Thus, leadership must be grounded in each of these aspects so that school administrators have the self-efficacy to address intergroup differences (Bell, 2002).

In the past, leadership focused on the promotion of diversity based on a social and moral justification (Combs, 2002). We contend that leadership models should propose more effective strategies to enhance issues of diversity in schools. We also believe that issues of diversity should encompass bottom-line leadership skills that sustain an ability to manage effectively and to improve organizational outcomes. Therefore, when leaders are given skills and confidence to perform effectively and appropriately in diversity situations, their inclination to persist despite adversity will assist the organization in problem identification and resolution (Combs, 2002). A leader's perception and confidence in successfully creating inclusive environments become important to eliminating the disparity between diversity training and diversity performance.

Unfortunately, there is limited research on which leadership models are beneficial in addressing issues of diversity in the workplace. There are also concerns over how a leader can develop a sense of self-efficacy to influence people's attitudes about diversity-related issues. In addition, we believe that leadership in diversity issues should be more than just promoting social and moral justification. While these are about effective change and diversity awareness, justification alone does not provide solutions to issues of leadership.

One can argue that in leading a diverse group of teachers and students, leaders must be knowledgeable about school participants' ethnic and cultural differences in order to ensure an inclusive school. Leaders must also understand the complexities of intergroup conflict and how power differences, inequality, and conflict originate from both identity and organization groups. Diversity perspectives pose challenges to many traditional beliefs in organization and management. Researchers have noted that diversity initiatives, such as valuing diversity, may have implications for how managers lead their organizations. Consequently, diversity perspectives may challenge present mainstream leadership theories as they recognize structural and cultural dimensions (Chen & Van Velsor, 1996). Thus, one can argue that developing skills of organizing and managing diverse employees falls in the domain of leadership. Questions surrounding leadership and organizational diversity have two forms, which might be characterized as "diverse leaders" versus "leadership of a diverse work force." These two aspects explore whether differences in sex, race, or ethnicity are associated with differences in the styles, patterns, or effects of leadership, as well as the type of leadership needed to use the talents and energies of a diverse work force.

The intersection of mainstream leadership theories and diversity research implies contrasting perspectives. Mainstream leadership theories and research conceive leadership at interpersonal and intrapersonal levels but rarely as having an intergroup focus. Mainstream leadership theories focus on the rational, purposeful, and goal-oriented leadership processes (Chemers & Murphy, 1995). In contrast, diversity research examines how social, racial, and cultural issues that originate outside the organizational boundaries affect leader–member interactions.

Therefore, mainstream theories define leadership in terms of personality characteristics and how the leader uses those abilities to influence his or her relationship with employees. Mainstream theories also do not look beyond the leader–follower relationship and how it affects identities in the workplace.

Diversity research has documented effects of race and gender on organizational networks, career opportunities, mentoring relations, employee perceptions, values, and communication styles (Cox, 1994; Chemers, Oskamp, & Costanzo, 1995; Chen & Van Velsor, 1996). Therefore, leaders who work with people from different ethnic backgrounds need to recognize cultural differences in their followers that may affect the ways in which relationships are developed and negotiated. Consequently, we need to recognize the importance of social group identity in leading diverse groups within the organization.

Unlike mainstream leadership theories, diversity research emphasizes group identities and views them as cultural identities. The concept of cultural identity can serve as a psychological lens through which to examine the experience and impact of diversity at the level of the individual precisely because it never loses its focus on the reality of group-level differences (Ferdman, 1995). The intercultural view that we are all cultural beings, shaped and oriented by the cultures of the groups to which we belong, addresses the dynamic implications for interpersonal and organizational processes and outcomes when members of different groups work together. This approach features looking at individuals in the context of their particular groups and being cognizant of and sensitive to their group membership (Mabokela & Madsen, 2003b; Madsen & Mabokela, 2000; Ferdman, 1995).

Research in the dynamics of cultural identity reveals that simply having some representatives of a particular ethnic group in an organization may not adequately leverage the potential for diversity. Diversity research brings into leadership training the importance of the subordinates' cultural identities and the need for leaders to understand how people are socialized and incorporated into the organization. The process of achieving inclusiveness may vary, depending on the cultural identity of the group. Furthermore, in developing and instituting mechanisms to facilitate socialization, we need to understand that the process of socialization works in relation to individuals and not just at the level of our collective construction of their groups as a whole (Madsen & Mabokela, 2000; Ferdman, 1995).

Diversity research perspectives pose challenges to many of the traditional assumptions of organization and management. Diversity initiatives and interventions emphasize group identities and view them as part of self-identities. Brickson (2000) believes that the identity orientations of minority and majority individuals within organizations have implications for how these individuals will be effective. Therefore, leaders who facilitate a relational identity orientation will promote the underlying factors necessary for a personalized and complex understanding of demographically different individuals on their own terms. Because an individual is motivated by others' welfare, both affective investment and trust are more likely to be evoked when group identities and self-identities interact positively (Brickson, 2000). A relational orientation in organizational contexts will result in more cooperation rather than competition, leading to deeper cognitive understanding and more positive affective and behavioral outcomes (Brickson, 2000).

In relation to understanding the importance of cultural identity in organizations, one must also understand intergroup differences. The dynamics of interaction between the members of different groups often can be understood in terms of the significance to individuals of the intergroup boundaries rather than in terms of any specific differences between groups (Triandis, 1995). Much work on ameliorating intergroup relations in organizations has focused on helping individuals work across group boundaries. This results in using approaches that move people beyond perceiving and treating each other as members of different groups, and to seeing them as individuals. People can relate in a variety of ways not only to other groups but also to their own. The mission for leaders is to understand how we can honor individual uniqueness and, at the same time, better explore and value group differences (Cox, 1994).

To explore these issues further, chapter 4 discusses findings from the first part of a two-part study exploring European American principals' perceptions of intergroup conflict and its implications for their leadership practices in creating inclusive schools. We examine how these leaders perceived and addressed intergroup conflict that resulted from cultural incongruity between European American participants and teachers of color. In chapter 5 we present part 2 of the leadership study, examining the perceptions of African American school leaders. We seek to understand how these leaders perceive intergroup conflict and its effect on their leadership practices. Based on the findings in our study, chapter 6 provides an overview of diversity self-efficacy and concluding thoughts on creating inclusive schools.

4
PRINCIPALS' PERCEPTIONS OF INTERGROUP CONFLICT: IMPLICATIONS FOR CREATING INCLUSIVE SCHOOLS

In this chapter we give a synopsis of how European American school leaders perceived and addressed intergroup conflict and how it created negative workplace relationships for teachers of color and European American school participants. Intergroup theory applies to school participants because of the nature of the organizational context between identity and organizational groups. We learned that leaders play a pivotal role in creating an inclusive school environment. These European American principals determined how group tensions would influence the emotional climate of the workplace and defined limited roles for the African American teachers.

Our findings revealed that the European American principals used what Lewis (2001) calls a "color-blind" approach, in which they avoided the racial realities and were unable to deal with racial undertones in their schools. In comparison, the African American principals (discussed later in this book) used a "color-conscious" process in which they acknowledged the salience of race in their interactions with other school participants. Acknowledging the contentious nature of this terminology, we use the term "color-conscious" as a way to define this leadership process, to characterize these administrators not by their race but by their willingness to put "color" always in the forefront of their administrative practices. We hope that eventually leaders will move from a "color-blind" to a "color-conscious" orientation in which the implications of race will be equitably addressed. Ultimately, we want "color-conscious" leadership to become a culturally conscious effort so that school participants are seen as individuals whose cultural identities are brought together to establish a relational identity orientation.

A Framework for Intergroup Conflict

Because a school reflects the diversity, classes, genders, socioeconomic statuses, and nationalities of its students, a complex set of interactions governs the formation of groups. Much has been written on how majority schools maintain a strong organizational culture through the process of selecting teachers. A dominant culture exists in these schools that imposes beliefs about appropriate ways of educating children. According to Lewis (2001), the fostering of a "color-blind" ideology allows most teachers to see themselves as racially neutral, deserving of their own success, and not responsible for the exclusion of others. Consequently, such schools have an organizational culture that does not reflect their diverse student bodies. The theoretical framework of intergroup theory is useful in understanding sources of conflict that occur in schools as a result of issues of diversity and the leaders' varying degrees of ability to establish an inclusive school culture.

Intergroup theory, leadership, and diversity are three areas that are invariably connected. Mainstream leadership theories view leadership at the intrapersonal (personality characteristics) and interpersonal (exchanges between leaders and followers) levels, but rarely at the intergroup level. When interactions between groups are implied, the focus is on the organizational group rather than on identity groups. In traditional hierarchical organizations composed of homogeneous groups, a leader may effectively lead a group because the values, needs, and expectations of the followers are similar. However, if leaders do not recognize the legitimacy of social identity in heterogeneous groups, they will not deal effectively with issues of gender, race, and other demographic dimensions. In contrast to mainstream leadership theory, diversity leadership perspectives look beyond leaders and followers and organizational identities to social, racial, and cultural issues outside organizational boundaries that affect leader–member interactions inside the organization (Chen & Van Velsor, 1996). Thus, intergroup theory in leadership research should provide a better understanding of the dynamics of diversity leadership.

According to Alderfer and Smith (1982), many organizations are composed of two types of groups: identity groups and organization groups. An identity group is a group whose members share common biological characteristics, have participated in equivalent historical experiences, were at times subjected to certain social forces, and hold similar worldviews (Alderfer & Smith, 1982; Nkomo & Cox, 1996). When people enter organizations, they bring their identity group identities based on variables such as ethnicity, sex, age, and family background. An organization group is one in which members share common organizational positions, participate in common work experiences, and have similar organizational views (Alderfer & Smith, 1982; Nkomo & Cox, 1996). An important factor in understanding intergroup relations in organizations is that membership in identity groups is not independent from membership in organizational groups: certain organizational groups tend to consist of members of particular identity groups.

Intergroup theory involves a complex set of interactions for understanding the effects of diversity of identities in the workplace (see appendix B). Identity group membership and organizational group membership are seen as highly related in their effects on social relations in organizations (Nkomo & Cox, 1996). When people of different subgroups interact with each other, there is an increased potential for intergroup conflict (Ayman, 1993). Such conflict is often viewed as negative because it requires majority workers to adjust their patterns of interaction with their minority counterparts. The leader strongly influences relations among groups, establishes the emotional climate of the workplace, determines how roles are structured, and plays a pivotal role in how intergroup conflict is addressed within the organization (Alderfer, 1977).

Sources of Intergroup Conflict

It is important to note that while research on intergroup theory in organizations has identified a number of characteristics that create opposing interests among groups, these sources of intergroup conflict are not dependent on particular groups or the specific setting in which the relationships occur (Alderfer & Smith, 1982). The analysis of intergroup relations is in part the study of power relations and in part the analysis of conflict among groups. Unequal power relationships occur when individuals who share a common condition induced by the actions of a high-power group form an association as a way to improve their status. Relations among groups may determine the effectiveness of the groups in achieving their objectives (Alderfer, 1977).

In the context of intergroup conflict there are conditions that influence how the leader and majority and minority groups will react to each other (Cox, 1994). A leadership model that recognizes the effects of power differences, inequality, and conflict that originate from both identity and organizational groups will assist leaders in negotiating, creating consensus, and building alliances among groups (Chen & Van Velsor, 1996). Various researchers have identified multiple sources of conflict and refer to how one condition of discord seems to affect another (Alderfer & Smith, 1982; Alderfer, Alderfer, Tucker, & Tucker, 1980; Cox, 1994). These properties include incompatible goals, competition for resources, cultural differences, power differences, conformity versus identity, group boundaries, affective patterns, cognitive formations, and leadership behavior. They often cause tensions between organizational and identity groups. (See appendix B for definitions of intergroup properties.)

European American Principals

European American principals faced multiple obstacles in leading and managing issues of diversity. While these were progressive principals who cared deeply about diversity, they were unable to conceptualize how a traditional organizational culture created barriers to inclusiveness.

These findings reveal that principals who are motivated on behalf of social justice and use antiracist leadership practices may still lack sufficient grounding in diversity leadership to establish an inclusive school. Riehl (2000) believes there are three administrative tasks that administrators need to consider in responding to children of color. She states that administrators should foster new meanings of diversity, promote an inclusive school culture and instructional programs, and build relationships between schools and communities. While these are worthwhile strategies, they do not examine how the principal should manage intergroup conflict that occurs at the organizational level.

An analysis of these European American principals' leadership practices and strategies revealed five properties of intergroup conflict: (1) an inability to gain goal consensus among the various school participants; (2) a hesitance to approach group boundaries and cultural differences among the African American and European American teachers; (3) a discomfort with using their power and influence to support African American teachers; (4) a lack of understanding about the importance of ethnic identity for the African American teachers; and (5) leadership struggles in establishing an inclusive school culture. (See appendices A and B for descriptions of intergroup conflict and themes.)

Incongruent Goals

In dealing with issues of diversity, various groups within a given organization may establish incongruent goals, which may result in intergroup tensions. The data analysis revealed that incongruent goals were held by the African American teachers and European American school participants. Thus, principals in this study struggled with how to develop goal consensus on issues of diversity between groups of school participants. Tensions due to these incompatible goals were apparent in these schools. The problem of incongruent goals resulted in (1) European American parents complaining about the amount of multicultural emphasis in African American teachers' classrooms; (2) European American teachers' concerns over the recruitment of African American teachers; and (3) European American participants' negative perceptions of African American teachers' roles on issues related to diversity.

Lewis's (2001) examination of how racial messages are perceived in homogeneous suburban schools suggests that school participants often used a color-blind approach to avoid confronting their own racist presumptions and understandings. Thus, as in this study, there were incongruent goals of establishing a schoolwide multicultural committee versus the parents' wishes to have less emphasis on these curricular areas. Parents in these schools did not value the role of "multiculturalism" in educating their children. Jane Frank had multiple complaints from parents who had children in the African American teachers' classrooms. She noted that she often had to defend the African American teachers and tell parents how fortunate they were to have these teachers and their multicultural focus. All the principals noted that tensions occurred when the school conducted schoolwide multicultural activities, as exemplified in this quote from Mary Jones:

> We don't make a big deal of Black History Month. We don't anymore. We make a big deal the whole year, and we try to spread things out so we don't do that. And our African American teacher was very clear with that. At one staff meeting she said, "I'm sick and tired of us talking about Black History Month." She said, "It's the shortest month of the year and it's the coldest month of the year." We've got to do stuff all year round. I mean, I get goose bumps when I think about that three years ago. Now that I look back, I get teary-eyed. It makes me understand how far we've come, but how much we need to do to observe multiculturalism. You know that we are pretty careful with the kinds of pictures we put up. We try to infuse as much as we can in the day-to-day. We try not make it too pronounced so parents will be happy.

Another incongruent goal among teachers of color and European American teachers was in the area of the recruitment and employment of teachers of color. All principals expressed their frustrations in building goal consensus among school participants in recruiting teachers of color to their schools. In Principal Jane Frank and Principal Mary Jones's schools, hiring decisions were made at the building level. Both principals noted heightened tensions between groups whenever a vacancy had to be filled. Often European American teachers expressed to both these principals their concerns that teachers of color might not be as qualified as they themselves were. This implied to the principals that European American teachers did not share their sentiments. Therefore, hiring decisions often made the African American teachers feel guarded in their responses to European American participants.

Jane Frank, who appeared to be the most outspoken about the importance of hiring teachers of color, could not get her European American teachers to agree with her. She felt their priorities were opposed to the hiring of another African American teacher. She noted:

> I had horrible battles with my team of teachers, but I look for visible minorities. And it has caused problems. I sent the African American teacher to help us out with hiring. She came back from the interviews and was pretty upset at the number of white females there.

Mary Jones expressed similar problems in achieving her school's recruitment goals. She stated that as a way to reduce the tensions, she established a hiring team that always had an African American teacher. It should be noted that the African American teacher on this team was also the only teacher of color at her school. While this practice placed undue hardship on the African American teacher, Mary Jones believed it was the only way she could develop goal consensus. Therefore, this administrative mandate fostered even greater conflict between the two groups of teachers. These tensions over recruitment often spilled over into other work-related matters, such as curriculum and instructional decisions. Mary Jones said that her European American teachers always stressed the importance of finding "qualified teachers," which resulted in hiring candidates who "must be like us":

> I was out in the open many times. I mean, I thought about what I was going to say before I said it. Other than this, I said, "This African American teacher is going to be on the hiring team." And I described what we should be looking for. I said, "We're going to be looking for quality, whoever that person is. That's whom we are going to hire." I said, "We're going to do a wide search so we can at least find some diversity. Whether it's male, whether it's colored, we're going to look."

Susan James said that at her school, hiring was centralized at the district level. In her district, the personnel director would provide her with a list of candidates to interview. Susan stated that when her mostly European American hiring team interviewed African American teachers, they were given closer scrutiny than prospective European American teachers. She also felt there were tensions about the "effectiveness" of African American teachers. She believed that her hiring team could have been more open in interviewing and evaluating prospective teachers of color. Susan noted the leadership challenges when these types of issues occurred at her school.

Another incongruent goal was related to how European American participants perceived African American teachers' roles at the school. The principals believed that the primary role for African American teachers was to educate European American teachers about issues related to diversity and to respond to the students of color. Unfortunately, this resulted in incongruent roles for African American teachers because the burden of cultural sensitization was placed on them. It became evident that these principals did not understand how this narrow definition of the African American teachers' competencies would result in European American teachers' viewing them as "tokens" and questioning their skills. Furthermore, these leadership decisions created more tensions about the role of teachers of color in these schools.

Jane Frank believed it was important for all of her students to have a positive African American role model. She felt that African American teachers should feel the same about their roles at the school. However, our discussions with the African American teachers revealed that they had conflicting feelings about their purpose and function in these schools. These incongruent goals between teachers of color and European American teachers about whose role it was to respond to issues of diversity created barriers to discussing these matters. Jane Frank noted that she and some of the other European American teachers had to convince teachers of color to come to and remain at the school:

I begged her [the African American teacher] to come. She wanted to teach in the city's schools. And I said, "You don't understand what you are doing here, and here is the rationale of why we need you more than the city's schools." And we did a rationale with her and what her role was here at the school. And we sat as a group [European American teachers] and explored the rationale with her to convince her that her being here would in effect have a more long-lasting range of effect for the global situation than her working immediately with kids. And that's how we got her here.

Cultural Differences and Group Boundaries

Cultural differences that occur in the workplace may result in tensions among and between groups. Due to cultural differences, group boundaries are manifested in such a way that the majority group makes decisions on what is acceptable and establishes the norms and expectations. Findings from this study revealed that through cultural differences, group boundaries were established between teachers of color and European American school participants. As a result of these group boundaries, these principals struggled in their leadership with how to address cultural differences. They noted the polarization of the feelings that European American teachers maintained against the African American teachers because of the cultural differences. While these principals noted there were negative feelings among the groups of teachers, they never addressed these group boundaries.

Our research (Madsen & Mabokela, 2000) on African American teachers in suburban school districts indicates that there is a tendency to limit the contributions of African American teachers to issues of race. Thus, teachers in these contexts become recognized only for their "Black expertise." In this study, principals expected African American teachers to assist them only with the hiring of teachers of color and to speak up at faculty meetings on issues that were related to African American students. Because of the principals' and school participants' limited knowledge about teaching children of color, African American teachers were placed in situations where they became the only voice for students of color. Therefore, African American teachers became role entrapped, with their value derived from their race and not their excellence as teachers. Because of cultural differences between African American and European American teachers, group boundaries were established, and principals were partly responsible for creating the limited role expectations for the teachers of color.

The principals exacerbated group tensions when they established hiring teams. As the "Black expert," principals identified the African American teacher as the lead person to provide know-how on recruiting other teachers of color. Principals believed they were establishing heterogeneous teams of teachers who would solve problems and share perspectives on recruiting diverse faculty. However, this group composition often resulted in a noncohesive team that would not communicate, could not agree on hiring criteria, and was ineffective. Thus, group boundaries were established, resulting in intergroup conflict in the team. While the principals realized that these hiring teams fostered tensions among the teachers, they themselves felt uncomfortable leading teacher teams on issues related to hiring teachers of color. By placing a teacher of color on each team, the principals abdicated their responsibility to address and resolve these challenging situations and, more important, to reinforce the value of diversity to their resistant European American teaching staff.

The ineffective responses of these principals to group boundaries call into question their own commitment to diversity. Were they hiring teachers of color only as a response to the city's desegregation plan, or did they believe in the meaningful value of these African American teachers' contributions? Analysis of the principals' interviews was quite telling. Their limited diversity perspectives made principals unwilling to address group boundaries among groups of teachers. They felt it was important to hire teachers of color, but they were unable to articulate to their staffs the value of hiring teachers of color. Mary Jones noted:

> That desegregation plan forced us to look at things, and we became the facilitators to help staff examine race and issues of bigotry. And if you don't elicit change as you hire teachers of color, you don't change. So I believe our view of integration is dependent on hiring, because that affects how other teachers [European Americans] think. I just think it is important that we get adults in the teaching profession involved, because it's so much to expect [African American] children to do the job of integration. They are the ones that pay the greatest price. The white adult group has reaped the benefits. We can learn from them [the children] and become better people because of it.

Additional group boundaries became apparent through cultural differences in instructional practices and placement decisions. Principals revealed that during placement decisions, the teacher teams often looked to the African American teacher to explain why a student of color was doing poorly at the school. It was apparent that the principals expected their African American teachers to be the sole persons responsible for the educational achievements of students of color. These leaders assumed that only the African American teachers needed to take ownership for the city's voluntary transfer students. By placing African American teachers on these teams, the principals basically absolved European American teachers from ensuring successful academic experiences for these students of color.

Because of the normative culture of these homogeneous suburban desegregated schools, teachers often used traditional instructional and classroom management practices. Discussions with the principals revealed that African American teachers' instructional practices were different from those of their European American peers. Each principal noted the success that African American teachers had with even the most challenging European American students. Principals often stated that because African American teachers were successful teachers, European American teachers often resented and were unwilling to listen to them. The following statement represents the principals' views on pedagogical differences:

> The African American teachers here are what I would call responsive teachers. If you go down the hallways, and I've been observing white teachers, you hear, "You have to respect me because I am the teacher." I have never heard that in the African American teacher's classroom. Yes, there are teacher differences here. What I've noticed is that the African American teacher does a lot of talking, but he teaches from the heart. The African American teacher's style is different from other [European American] teachers. I think the [European American] teachers become so frustrated in working with him. He is really successful with students. And at times, I think they resent him for it. I can't think of a time that I have seen the African American teacher doing a straight lecture without interaction with the kids. I mean there is always dialogue going back and forth. That

teacher [African American] is not like the other teachers, where they force students to listen.

Group boundaries became apparent with parents and students, who often challenged the African American teachers' curriculum decisions and instructional practices. Principals stated their frustrations with trying to be responsive to parents, yet ensuring that the African American teacher's concerns were met. Jane Frank noted that one time the African American teacher came to her regarding the parent of one of her students. This teacher felt that the parent held racist beliefs toward her. Jane noted that she did nothing and, as a result, the African American teacher lashed out at her. She stated that at times she was clueless on whether parents were racist or not. Jane felt she was not as responsive as she could be to her African American teachers:

> A parent was critical of the African American teacher. I am upfront and spoke with her about it. She [the African American teacher] felt that I had not supported her because I was listening to the parent. So her view of my role was to support her. In communicating with the African American teacher, I determined that the parent did have racist attitudes about her, and she felt I didn't jump on it.

Power Differences

Power differences between majority and minority members of an organization are the most problematic of group conflict conditions. The organizational culture has both a direct and an indirect impact on the allocation of power among diverse groups. The values and ideologies in organizational cultures determine what behaviors will be reinforced. Individuals with power define the organization's culture, determine which groups get power, and define the very nature of power (Ragins, 1995). Findings from this study revealed that these principals were unclear on how power differences between the teachers of color and the European American school participants created disharmony in their schools. It was evident that these principals did not use their authority to minimize power differences between groups on instructional issues and staff development.

Findings from this study revealed that these principals struggled with power differences in responding to both groups on establishing an organizational direction on diversity issues. They did not use their influence to create a more open and honest dialogue between the two groups of teachers about deficient expectations for students of color and using more culturally relevant instructional practices. Principals noted that some of the staff development programs did promote diversity, but they were unable to identify and address cultural differences between the two groups of teachers. There were power differences between the European American and African American teachers on decisions made about staff development needs, discipline of students of color, and recruitment issues. Principals were hesitant to facilitate a dialogue among teachers about these issues. They did not feel comfortable addressing racial undertones that were generated during faculty meetings and staff development meetings in response to the needs of students of color.

Principals also could have used their authority to minimize power differences between European American parents and African American teachers. They stated several times how problematic parents were in dealing with the African American teachers and how unhappy they were with the amount of diversity in their classrooms. Jane Frank often said that parents approached her weekly with their concerns about her African American teachers' selections of multicultural classroom readings.

While these principals felt their superintendents were supportive of their authority to hire teachers of color, they also felt the burden of dealing with parents' complaints. Principals Mary Jones and Susan James were not as willing to be as outspoken on issues of diversity because of the number of parent complaints that occurred. Jane Frank, who was the most assertive in addressing parent complaints, made it clear to them that complaints about the African American teachers would not be tolerated. She used her authority to diminish power differences, but only because of the board's support:

> To tell you the truth, a parent came in and made a comment that they did not want a Black teacher. I asked them to leave. I would not deal with them, but not because I am so virtuous.

My superintendent would not ask me to support what I could not do, and he would never condone that. Our board also would not support that either.

Susan James said she went to great lengths, in attempting to minimize power differences, to convince European American parents that the African American teacher was competent. She mentioned that she often had to convince European American parents that the African American teacher was exceptional and had a record of success with disruptive children. Susan felt her parents' complaints were not valid because she believed that the African American teacher in her building was more effective than other teachers. She stated that she often went into detail about the African American teacher's pedagogical practices and how the parents' children would benefit from them. Similarly, she noted that her European American parents never questioned her in such detail about the European American teachers' pedagogical practices.

Principals did not use their leadership in ways that could have minimized power differences between African American teachers and European American school participants. These principals realized the important role that their African American teachers played in supporting their districts' goals of participating in the desegregation program. But, unfortunately, they seemed to consider using their influence and power to improve the working conditions for teachers of color and to put an end to parents' and teachers' complaints about diversity too risky. In many ways, there were missed leadership opportunities to change school practices that would support the recruitment and retention of teachers of color.

Identity Censorship

Managing intergroup conflict is often based on how minorities feel their group identity will be preserved and how responsive the majority group is in supporting them. The leader plays an important role in managing the tensions of minority group workers, who are often expected to conform in order to preserve the homogeneous microculture of the organization (Ferdman, 1995). Findings from this study revealed how the organizational culture of these schools negatively affected African American teachers and their relationships with European American school participants. The conflict of identity censorship may have manifested itself in African American teachers' isolating themselves from others. Principals in this study mentioned several times their concerns about the withdrawal of African American teachers from social situations. These principals failed to understand the importance of African American teachers' ethnic identity and how identity censorship may have affected their psychological well-being.

These principals said that they were concerned when their African American teachers would withdraw to their classrooms during lunch or when they did not attend school social functions. It was evident that the principals' expectation for social involvement was placed on the shoulders of African American teachers. Principals stated that the European American teachers were not as responsive and open to the African American teachers as they could have been. Though these principals observed the limited voice of the African American teachers and their isolation, they did not seek out the reasons why these teachers felt silenced by the constraints of their school culture.

Principals Mary Jones and Jane Frank were concerned about how withdrawn the African American teachers were. Mary observed that isolation was a way for the African American teacher to protect herself:

> The African American teacher may isolate herself because of her race sometimes, just to protect herself and keep her focused. Other teachers will do the same thing just to survive in a profession. Do you know what I am saying? There is a different reason for doing it, and I can't understand why she does.

Susan James also noted the social isolation of the African American teacher in her building, but was unclear regarding the reason:

> I don't know why, because I don't think he should be surprised that he is well liked and highly thought of. Yet, he does seem surprised. He thinks that somehow the things that teachers do for other people are somehow not for him. I don't know why … I am not sure. We talked about his mom and some of those connections, and yet, I don't know.

These principals did not identify how the expectation for conformity and the traditional school culture resulted in censoring these teachers' identities. They may have misunderstood how this intergroup conflict created a negative environment for teachers of color. This suppression resulted in African American teachers needing affirmation of their identity through their classroom multicultural activities and the use of culturally relevant pedagogical practices. Thus, this need of the African American teachers to preserve their identities created even more tensions. It was evident that these principals did not value their African American teachers' need for self-preservation and did not realize how insensitive other school participants were to them.

Leadership Behavior

The last property of intergroup conflict is leadership and the influence it has in establishing conflict between organizational and identity groups. The role of the leader in a network of intergroup relations determines the intensity of group conflicts (Alderfer, 1977). The cultural differences, cognitive formations, and conformity pressures made it apparent that these principals were troubled with how to establish a leadership style that was responsive to the tensions existing between the groups of teachers. In fact, these principals were often the conduit to creating more tensions because they did not understand how their leadership established these group tensions and boundaries in their schools.

In examining their leadership and responding to intergroup tensions, these principals noted that they were inadequately prepared to "mend fences" and respond to the racial tensions in their buildings. They were conflicted about how to lead discussions about racial and cultural differences with their teachers. They struggled with balancing everyone's needs. They viewed diversity as a negative and did not value it as a way to improve the conditions for children of color, as this quote reflects:

> One group doesn't want diversity and the other side is What is diversity? And the staff here is saying behind my back, "She's on a kick for hiring African American teachers, she really believes that you have to do this, and what about all of these other qualified people?"

Principals grappled with their ability to lead in dealing with the politics of race. They struggled with balancing African American and European American parents' needs. European American parents' concerns were about too much exploration of multicultural issues, their children's interactions with children of color, and having an African American teacher. On the other side, African American parents came to them about their children's needs. Their issues centered on the low expectations for their children by European American teachers, long bus rides to take African American students to and from school, safety concerns, and the need for more teachers of color. This quote from Jane Frank expresses her frustrations in working with both groups of parents:

> There are times when I have to tell parents that they just have to live with it. I have to live with it myself. When the desegregation plan started, we did not know what the heck was going on. Parents called. I told them if they did not like what was happening at the school, they could call the board. I told the parent her child was lucky, and to let her child soak it up.

Another leadership area that emerged was recruitment and retention of teachers of color. Principals struggled with where to find "qualified" African American teachers. They wanted only teachers of color who would "fit into their school culture." Mary Jones felt strongly that she did not want a "militant Black" teacher because he or she would upset the European American teachers. Principals were also concerned about how a teacher of color would interact with parents and maintain the school's academic focus. The key word was "qualified," which became code for "be like us" in dress, use of language, and philosophy. Jane Frank reflected:

> We had a Black teacher interview here, but her degree was in African American studies. I am not sure that at this stage the [European American] staff is ready for that. I think we might go a different way. So this past year we interviewed another Black teacher and eventually hired her. Her speech was impeccable. She had very, very fine English skills. Her dress was impeccable, and she was laid back. But she had a harder time here than the

other African American teachers. Even though this teacher would bring a better gift to this school, the staff still created problems for her. They were just awful to her.

Another leadership obstacle was the principals' discomfort with how to interact with the African American teachers. The principals stated that they had had limited exposure to people of color and often had to face the stereotypes they held about African Americans. Their African American teachers were not happy at the school and at times had secluded themselves. In light of their limited contacts with people of color, principals were not aware of the complexity of racial identity and how this may have affected the African American teachers. These principals stated that it was difficult to change the culture and the mind-set of school participants:

> We recently hired another African American teacher. I decided to put her in the same grade level as the other African American teacher there. She [African American teacher] was so excited about her coming on board, she was not threatened. The African American teacher said she was looking forward to this teacher as a way to charge her up. I didn't say anything, but you know, I realized she needed another African American teacher to charge her up.

Conclusion

The preceding discussion has highlighted the important role that European American principals played in managing intergroup conflict in schools where teachers of color are in the minority. These findings revealed there were multiple sources of intergroup conflict that created a negative environment for the promotion of diversity and for teachers of color. This study also noted the important role the principal plays in understanding and solving these conflicts. The leadership of these administrators exacerbated the formation of incongruent goals among the school groups that resulted in group boundaries and cultural differences among the school participants. Findings from this study implied that European American principals were unsure about how to lead on issues of diversity, thus causing teachers of color to withdraw. These boundaries also affected European American teachers' unwillingness to be responsive to students of color and created a "color-blind talk" on issues related to race.

It is important for leaders to understand how organizational groups and identity groups relate to each other. By identifying areas of intergroup conflict, we can help leaders understand the important role they play in reducing the perceived negative benefits of diversity in their schools. Increasing diversity by hiring teachers of color may result in the formation of subgroups, which increases intergroup boundaries and competition. When intergroup interactions are implied, the usual focus is more on the organizational group and not on the identity group. Diversity leadership perspectives look beyond leaders and followers to social, racial, and cultural issues outside organizational boundaries that affect leader–member interactions in the organization (Chen & Van Velsor, 1996).

5

AFRICAN AMERICAN LEADERS' PERCEPTIONS OF INTERGROUP CONFLICT

Introduction

In chapter 4 our discussion examined how European American principals' leadership created intergroup tensions between teachers of color and European American school participants that established an exclusive environment. In this chapter, we explore how African American school leaders' understandings of cultural differences were used to create inclusive environments. We seek to understand how African American leaders perceive intergroup conflict as it affects their ability to lead, and to acknowledge the challenges that African American school administrators face in leading a group of predominantly European American school participants.

An analysis of leaders' perceptions and their relation to their leadership revealed four themes that were recognized as properties of intergroup conflict (as discussed in chapter 4): (1) incompatible goals of the principals and various school constituents; (2) problems of group boundaries in how they dealt with European American teachers' cultural differences; (3) power struggles and how they affected their interactions with teachers, parents, and other school administrators; and (4) the development of a "color-conscious" leadership in working with European American and African American teachers.

Incompatible Goals

Leaders of color who interact with multiple groups must deal with a constituency that may not be supportive of them (Chemers, 1993). Research reveals that followers' perceptions of a leader of color are often checked against prototypes. That is, leaders of color undergo scrutiny to determine their capabilities and professional contributions. Consequently, there are concerns about how minorities in majority organizations are promoted to leadership positions. Cox (1994) contends that in organizations, properties of intergroup conflict will influence how the leader and majority and minority members will perceive and respond to each other.

Various groups within a given organization may develop incompatible goals when dealing with issues of diversity, which results in intergroup tensions. Our data analysis revealed that African American school administrators in our study struggled with how to respond to incompatibility between their goals and those of European American school participants. It was apparent that these school administrators were unable to shift the mind-set of their school participants to accept diversity in these schools. The incompatibility of goals and subsequent tensions experienced by these school leaders emanated from the following areas: (1) the lack of commitment on the part of their schools to recruit teachers of color; (2) the lack of focus on the importance of diversity for both African American and European American students; (3) their place as role models for both African American and European American students; and (4) the need for the assistant principals to prove their worth within their schools.

The African American school leaders noted incompatible goals in their schools' lack of commitment to hire teachers of color. They eloquently expressed the importance that teachers of color played in the lives of all the students. Yet, they met with resistance in their efforts to move their schools in this direction. These school administrators stated that their district often told them that they could not find "qualified" minority candidates. The male participants at both the elementary and the secondary level noted that there was no district commitment at all to recruit teachers of color. Most agreed that their districts had not identified specific strategies for minority teacher recruitment. It appeared that if people of color did apply, they were always met with a degree of hesitancy. The participants also noted that their districts were unclear on how to recruit teachers of color, yet made little effort to assess the strategies they were using. This meant that personnel directors went to teacher education programs only at predominantly white universities and did not consider recruiting at historically Black institutions.

Of all the participants, Ralph Green was the most vocal in his attempts to get his district to recruit teachers of color. Ralph stated that when positions were advertised, he often identified several "qualified candidates" of color. But he believed that his district put them through such intense scrutiny that it lost many candidates. Thus, he was often disappointed when he would review how many teachers of color were hired, given the large numbers of available teaching positions:

> We approached our district with a list of minority newspapers, Black colleges, and all the Black fraternal organizations to recruit. Well, this year I made phone calls to minority candidates from the Historically Black Colleges and Universities (HBCUs). Of the eight who applied, only one was hired. Why weren't the others hired? I mean, they [principals in other schools] made the minority applicants go four or five times for interviews before they were hired. It's discriminatory. They have not made a commitment to hiring Black, minority people. They don't like to hear it, but I'll tell them that. I am constantly reminding them of that. I think if they had a choice, they wouldn't hire them at all.

The female African American assistant principal, Maxine Boyd, had a different perspective on her district's hiring practices for teachers of color. She believed that her district's commitment to hire teachers of color was in part due to the "vocal" African American parents who lived in the district. She believed it was an "appeasement" factor, where administrators provided "lip service" but never changed their personnel practices. When the district did hire teachers of color, she believed they were hired only to teach "safe subjects," such as music and vocational classes. She also noted that her district was hesitant to hire teachers from the city schools because they "brought too much baggage" with them:

> This is a community where the minority population is growing. This is a community that is vocal. I have seen appeasement. I have seen minorities hired in areas that are nonthreatening, such as the fine arts, vocational classes, or, in one instance, we have one at the lower level in foreign language. Of course, none of them at the high school level. They feel that a Black coming in from the city brings certain baggage. This is just my perception; no one has verbalized this. They feel that Blacks from the city talk a certain way that wouldn't be acceptable with kids here. The community is very involved, and there is a lot of pressure on who is hired and who is not. I have seen Black teachers come and go here.

Another area of incompatibility was in their schools' and districts' commitment to issues of diversity, their lack of understanding of African American students' needs, and the compelling need to hire "role models" for these students. All of the participants believed that they always had to make issues of diversity and the focus on African American students a priority. All of the male African American participants stated the importance of having "Black males" at the school to assist in promoting positive images for their male African American students. However, David Main, at the high school level, was more frustrated because he believed his presence as the "school's Black male" often jeopardized his relations with these students. While he was able to negotiate effectively with the African American students, he felt the distinct risk of alienating the other school participants. However, like the other participants, he felt a strong sense of conscience in needing to reach out and help the students of color:

> Most of the African American students here are in the basic level courses. They are perceived to be the behavioral problems of the school. They are looked at as the kids who are not willing to deal with assimilation, that is the perception. I am talking in

generalities. The problem is, at the high school level there is not much I can do....I have been asked, being in suburban districts for the past five years, to save Black boys. I think what happens is people see me work with Black boys who are on the right track and I am able to influence where those kids are going.

While Maxine Boyd noted the importance of "role models" as well, she was also concerned about the lack of activities for the African American students to promote a sense of cultural identity. She believed not only that role models are important, but also that African American students need additional support through school activities and special events. When it came to Black History Month, she was the only person who willingly accepted this responsibility:

> There is a lack of role models here. Role models stimulate self-esteem. Self-esteem enhances learning. It is not that a Black teacher or a white teacher can teach better. It is that a child sees someone who looks like them. They have a club [for African American students] here that brings in programs throughout the year. I am the only one who does things for the Black students here. During Black History Month, if I did not do anything, no one would. No one here knows what to do for the Black students here.

Another area of incompatibility for these African American leaders was their own feelings of self-conflict. In dealing with multiple cultural identities, these participants struggled with the complexity of race and its implications for their ability to lead. They often noted that their legitimacy was questioned and they were asked whether they were going to be loyal to school participants' collective interests or promote an ambivalent relationship with the African American students. While they attempted to project an image highly consistent with that of their European American participants, they also were conflicted over how to respond to and be perceived by African American students.

Most of the participants felt that their color and its meaning became problematic when they were promoted to principal. The African American leaders were cognizant of the fact that they had to avoid compromising themselves while having to negotiate the organizational ladder in order to be promoted. Ralph Green and Roger Winter noted that their districts were not willing to promote "Blacks" to principals. They believed that majority school participants (although it was unacknowledged) viewed them as cultural brokers who bridged the gap between the African American students and the district. These African American principals were valued for their ability to sensitize their European American colleagues about racial matters. Therefore, because of their importance in enlightening school participants on these issues and because there were too few African Americans in these positions, they were at risk for not being promoted. In essence, they felt that just coming in and working hard and waiting to be promoted was not enough. They constantly had to fight stereotypes about their professional abilities. As Ralph Green noted:

> The superintendent brought in all these people, white females, whom he hired. Even though you know you are well regarded by teachers and parents, you can't get hired. And when you go to these district meetings, I am always wondering if I measure up. Do I measure up? So there's always this measuring yourself against those yardsticks. Because you're always assuming that others are measuring you with that stick, too. We go to these meetings and there are thousands of school administrators and only five Blacks. It just makes me wonder.

As cultural brokers working with both students of color and European American students, the assistant principals wanted to be perceived as administrators who were more central to the mission of the school. Yet, they found themselves having to balance the conflict that occurred with within-group and between-group processes in terms of how they handled discipline of European American and African American students. David Main was caught up in how he disciplined the students at his high school. On the one hand, his European American students perceived him as a "token" who was not fair in his discipline practices. Yet, the African American students thought he was harder on them:

> I view myself as an advocate for Black students. I have to be. I also view myself as a role model for [European American] students who may be fearful in dealing with Black males. No other school administrator needs to view themselves in that way.

I think those are two special things I need to keep in mind. I need to be an advocate for Black students, and if I don't do it, nobody else will. But I also need to be fair to all my students here.

Cultural Differences and Group Boundaries

Cultural differences in the workplace may result in tensions among and between groups. Through cultural differences, group boundaries are manifested where the majority group makes decisions on what is acceptable and establishes the norms and expectations. Findings from this study revealed that cultural differences led to conflicts between the African American school administrators and European American school participants. These cultural differences were manifested in two ways: first, in how various school constituents perceived these leaders and, second, in how they interacted with teachers regarding their instructional practices, expectations, and stereotypes they held about African American students.

All of the participants expressed "image management" concerns. Chemers and Murphy (1995) note that when persons of color enter into a leadership position in a mostly homogeneous organization, they often face misperceptions by followers who question their effectiveness as leaders. Because perceptions are susceptible to bias and distortion, it becomes important to recognize that trust and competence will impact the leader's ability to get followers to attain goals. Thus, these principals felt that due to negative perceptions held by their European American colleagues, they often spent much time and energy having to socially construct their professional roles before they could focus on one-on-one leader–member relationships of trust and reciprocity.

In some ways, Ralph Green at the elementary school noted his image management concerns more than his secondary school counterparts. He spent a disproportionate amount of time explaining his leadership decisions to his European American colleagues. He lamented:

> There was a conception when I was hired that they had to hire someone Black. There's no doubt in my mind that the committee held stereotypes about me. In terms of parents, I had no

problems, because they knew I was serious. But with the staff, I had conflict. They were pretty arrogant about me being in here.

The other principals experienced similar reactions from their school participants, as well as the amount of time they had to spend in developing an inclusive relationship. This meant being open-minded in their personal and work-related actions, in order to reduce the anxiety and uncertainty among school participants. By being inclusive, they believed they gained the respect of staff, which then allowed them to address cultural differences. In many ways, these participants felt they were often misperceived and encapsulated in certain roles. Maxine Boyd in particular noted her struggles in working with school participants:

> Demanding respect for my position, having to prove myself—that I am capable of this job—is always in my mind. Having to work and at the same time watch out of the corner of my eye so that they will not sabotage my efforts. Or set me up for failure. I am making sure that I am not labeled as a disciplinarian, because a Black administrator can be labeled as a disciplinarian. That means you don't have any smarts, just know-how to make kids behave. It is not a complimentary position.

These participants noted that part of their leadership role was to work with European American teachers concerning their own cultural differences with the African American students. These leaders of color cited the important role they played in "turning around" teachers in reference to their pedagogical practices and instructional decisions. At the elementary level, these discussions with European American teachers were always at the forefront of Ralph Green's leadership. He often assisted European American teachers with how to interact with African American parents and encouraged them to have high expectations for students of color. He would not let these teachers operate on a deficit model in working with the students of color:

> We would at times have African American kids who came in from the city, who were at times dirty. Teachers tended to push them away. And the kids can read it, and I hate teachers for that. So, therefore, for these children it is how they are perceived or

viewed. These teachers have a lot to learn, coming in here from their white, middle-class homes and cultural expectations. They are teaching in the unknown with those kids from different backgrounds. They just haven't learned how to bring those kids to where they should be. In other words, they pity them, you know, "poor little guy." This is what I work with.

The administrators at the high school level focused more on how cultural differences manifested themselves in the way children of color were tracked into their high school programs. These participants noted that European American teachers perceived African American students as inferior because of their language. As a result, the students were disproportionately placed in the lower, nonacademic tracks. Mr. Winter stated:

> We use a test in the eighth grade. The African American students are placed in certain tracks. More than likely those kids remain in those tracks. Only if parents challenge the tracking does something get done. The majority of white students go into the upper tracks, and our minority students are at the lower tracks. When they [African American students] come to us, they are in the basics track. Only 7 percent are in the upper tracks.

Maxine Boyd also noted the intergroup conflict of getting European American participants to change their cultural beliefs about African Americans. She believed these teachers' "color-blindness" resulted in their not addressing the racial realities that surrounded them. She asserted that the European American teachers' stereotypes about African Americans were so embedded that it would be difficult to change these beliefs:

> You have people here who know nothing of the African American culture. Nor do they wish to learn. And you still have people here who will always say, "I am not reflecting on where they come from." I always say they have a South African mentality. You will always have them thinking that Blacks are inferior. They can be really smart Black children, but they are still Black, so therefore, they are inferior.

Power Differences

Power differences between majority and minority members of an organization are the most problematic intergroup conflict conditions. Individuals with power define the organization's culture, determine which groups get power, and state the very nature of power. However, leaders of color in managerial positions often reported having less job discretion and feeling less accepted than white managers (Greenhaus, Parasuraman, & Wormley, 1990). Ethnic differences between leader and followers may result in exchanges that can be detrimental to the organization's goals (Chemers & Murphy, 1995).

All of the participants said that because of their positions of authority, they often grappled with how participants responded to their leadership. Each participant noted that certain school groups challenged his or her leadership. The power differences were manifested in two ways: first, European American teachers' dismissal of the administrators' authority to change their instructional practices for students of color and, second, European American teachers' and other administrators' misconception of the principals as "tokens" with little real power.

At the elementary level, Ralph Green noted that the power differences were more pronounced in his dealings with the European American teachers. He believed his role as instructional leader was to make teachers who were not culturally responsive to students of color aware of their pedagogical practices and expectations. Many times, he had to address discipline inequities to ensure that African American students were treated fairly. In his interactions with teachers, they resented his authority and often dismissed his suggestions. He believed that teachers were even more resentful when he served as an advocate for the students of color:

> It took a while to turn it around here. As an administrator it was very difficult [for European American teachers] to accept taking directions from or be supervised by a Black person. The truth is, the teachers and I had a lot of problems. Whenever anything happened, they looked at the Black child and not the white child. We would have staff meetings and I would try to get these teachers to change. So there was this big difference here. But I think it took a person who wasn't afraid to confront those issues.

By being Black, I certainly had had my share of those incidents and needed to communicate that to staff.

At the secondary level, teachers perceived these leaders as "tokens" with little authority. Participants cited conflicting demands of dealing with faculty who saw them only in a certain role and based their perceptions on their own stereotypes. Like Ralph Green, they noted their struggles with teachers, but often felt powerless to get teachers to change. David Main said:

> By the third year, the staff finally warmed up to me. In dealing with the faculty, I have had positive ones. I have had some negative ones as well. The unfortunate thing is, there is not much I can do to change the [European American] teachers' minds.

Two of the secondary participants recounted their power struggles in dealing with their administrative peers. They found that often their leadership was questioned when they went beyond their expertise on racial matters. Though in a power position, they were concerned that much of their energy was being spent having to validate their place and competence in these schools. Given their leadership role, they often faced situations where their authority was questioned because of their color. These principals struggled with power differences, always being questioned about who they were and what they represented. As Roger Winter put it:

> I knew our principal didn't truly respect me for who I was. I think he was happy that I was there. I cut down on the confusion and kept the Black students in line. But I don't think he respected me. I think after they watched me for a while, they respected me. That doesn't mean that we're going over to each other's houses to eat. They have had little exposure to people like me. They don't know how to act, and then there are the condescending statements, like "You're very articulate."

Leadership Behavior

Leadership and the influence it has on how organizational and identity groups interact is critical to understanding intergroup conflict. Culturally based stereotypes and expectations of majority followers may influence how they interact with minorities in leadership positions. Therefore, the problem minority leaders have is that they may have values, attitudes, traits, and behaviors that are contrary to beliefs traditionally held by the majority group (Chemers & Murphy, 1995). These leaders used their authority to confront intergroup conflicts between themselves and other school participants. This could be seen in their ability to develop a color-conscious leadership style that recognized cultural differences among school participants and in their willingness to address racial undertones.

All of the leaders said that in leading their school participants, it became apparent that they had to incorporate the connections and interrelations among the various groups. Therefore, with each group of school participants, whether it was teachers, parents, or students, these administrators soon developed a "color-conscious" leadership style. They stated that one of their roles was to understand the meaning and implications of being an outsider, yet behaviorally they had to be flexible in order to lead their traditional organizations. Developing a color-conscious ability was important for them to remain in these settings. As stated by Roger Winter:

> Everything that occurs at this school is racial. It's simply situational. But if you deal with it as racial, you need to point out things. Those kinds of things have to happen. As a leader, I learned all of the fears and concerns that teachers have about these kids and how that affects my decisions. Don't have people wondering what you are saying, and speak like an intellect. That is the language they understand here. In this environment, you have to be a leader who can interact with all the differences.

Each leader, in different ways, described the significance of his or her relationship with European American and African American students. They stated that while their exchanges and responses varied as they interacted with various group-level cultures, they were all equally important. For the European American students, it was more about dispelling stereotypes in their interactions with this group. In leading a homogeneous school, many noted the need to assert their authority so they would be perceived as competent.

Because these principals used a color-conscious leadership style, they were able to address intercultural contact between groups and understood how to navigate between the two cultures without losing their identity. These leaders developed an intercultural relationship with both their identity group and the dominant group; that is, they could adapt their leadership to respond to the needs of all of the school participants. By being able to move between the cultural identities of the school participants, they had an understanding of within-group as well as between-group processes.

Because of their group-level racial understandings, they believed their leadership with African American students took on another level of interaction. In leading African American students, these administrators noted that they wore many hats. Their leadership focused on being "mom," strengthening these students' identity, and serving as a racial advocate. While in many ways these participants addressed their concerns of needing to be fair in their leadership practices, they felt the tensions of having to balance how other school participants perceived them. They were strong in their commitment and were willing to make additional efforts for students. Maxine Boyd put it thus:

> Being a Black administrator in an all-white environment with a few Black kids, it's like being a mom where you don't have a role. Sometimes my Black kids will come in and I will tell them "which hat am I wearing?" I tell them they have to wear a belt, and they can't wear their pants like that. When one will come in and they are crying, I say, "Do I need my 'girlfriend hat' on today?"

Through their color-conscious leadership, these principals made concerted efforts to hold teachers accountable for the "deseg" students at their schools. In particular, these participants mentioned the conflicting relationships they had when they interacted with teachers about the students of color. These relationships were strained by the way these leaders pushed a leadership style that forced teachers to examine their own "color-blind" approaches with students. In general the participants noted that they often pressed the European American teachers to hold high expectations and to treat the African American students fairly. As said by Maxine Boyd:

I think leadership to [European American] teachers is dependent on how they deal with children and the expectations they hold for them. If you have a sense of equity in the classroom, then everyone should be responsible. Teachers' body language tells a lot to the students here. And if there is a situation, I will not hesitate to bring it to the teachers' attention. I have high standards and am pretty vocal about things.

Conclusion

In this chapter we have examined the important role leaders of color play in leading and in managing sources of conflict in suburban desegregated schools. This study revealed multiple sources of intergroup conflict that affected their leadership decisions. There were incompatible goals among the school groups that resulted in group boundaries and cultural differences among the school participants. Because of these group boundaries, the assistant principals struggled with power differences and what they meant in leading and facilitating intercultural contact between and among identity and organizational groups.

For organizations to be effective, all groups of leaders must understand how organizational groups and identity groups relate to each other. The African American administrators in this study had an understanding of how to address the two-way nature of intercultural contact between groups and understood how to move back and forth among and between the identity groups of their school participants. Leaders of color face multiple challenges in how majority followers will respond to their authority. They have to understand the cultural variations among groups of followers and how they will influence their effectiveness.

Further research needs to be conducted to examine how principals of color negotiate boundaries of race in suburban contexts. Much could be learned about their color-conscious approach to ensure equitable practices for all schoolchildren. Few studies have examined leaders of color in suburban contexts; therefore, the emergence of leadership influence structures and their effects on intergroup conflict among minority and majority school participants, and the role of race and ethnicity in this process needs additional investigation.

Clearly, the research findings would cause one to carefully examine the variety of skills that leaders of color must employ in creating an inclusive school for all students. By promoting a "color-conscious" leadership in these contexts, these African American administrators may provide insights on what skills are needed to understand within-group as well as between-group processes. As noted in the findings, these leaders were able to move between the cultural identities and incorporate the connections and interrelationships among the groups.

Although this was an exploratory study, findings from this research might have implications for preparing principals in how to respond to intergroup conflict. According to Chen and Van Velsor (1996), bicultural identity of people of color is often an undervalued strength within the organization. Having a bicultural identity may enable leaders to move back and forth between cultural expectations and norms of two or more cultures. Therefore, leaders become cultural integrators and facilitators in creating common ground among groups.

Emerging literature on global leadership implies that leaders can no longer focus on task and organizational goals only (Chen & Van Velsor, 1996). In motivating a diverse group of followers, leaders must build a one-on-one leader–member relationship in which they create and facilitate new meaning out of diverse viewpoints. Therefore, we need to identify leaders who can tolerate ambiguity among the group identities, and develop inclusive skills, cultural sensitivity, and a global mind-set.

Given that the demographics of our schools are rapidly changing, one of the most important findings from our study was that these African American leaders had a "color-conscious" leadership that allowed them to move back and forth between groups. They appeared to have a broad view, so they were able to handle intergroup tensions and facilitate new boundaries in finding common ground among the participants. Thus, they were behaviorally flexible enough to enhance school participants' awareness in responding to the African American students. Though these leaders often struggled with their followers' image management of them, they were able to develop an open-minded learning orientation despite those perceptions.

Our findings revealed that these administrators were able to move from their own cultural group to work with these school participants. Consequently, their followers benefited as these administrators took responsibility for dispelling stereotypes and proved they were competent leaders. As African American leaders, they developed the capacity to be open-minded, continuous learners, relationship builders, and people developers. These "color-conscious" leaders were cultural integrators and consensus builders who had acquired a great deal of understanding about the diversity of groups and were able to establish leader–member trust. Whether the result of their ethnic backgrounds or their leadership capabilities, these skills are critical in leading heterogeneous groups in responding to the needs of all students.

Profiles of African American School Leaders

Roger Winter grew up in an urban neighborhood and attended an integrated school until the fifth grade. Elementary school was an academically successful experience for him because the competition in his classes kept him focused on his studies. Upon completion of his elementary schooling, he was bused to a predominantly homogeneous European American school. During high school, he had positive interactions and friendships with European American students. Upon graduation, he pursued his baccalaureate studies at a predominantly European American university. He studied journalism in college and became a sportswriter for a local paper upon graduation. After several years, he grew "tired of this position." In his quest to "give back and work with African American children," Mr. Winter explored the possibility of coaching or substitute teaching. However, he was unable to secure a position in these areas. The personnel director recruited Mr. Winter to teach in a suburban school district. After teaching high school English for approximately 6 years, he was invited to apply for an administrative position where he would be responsible for student management. Though he has played an important role in assisting African American students to navigate the maze of desegregated schooling, Mr. Winter expressed concerns about his own future in the district, especially with regard to opportunities for promotion.

Ralph Green was the only elementary assistant principal participating in this study. He received his elementary and high school education at mostly European American schools. After completing high school, Mr. Green served in the military for 4 years. After his military experience, he attended a historically Black institution, where he received his teacher preparation. Mr. Green began his teaching career in his current suburban school district. He taught in the district for 12 years before he was invited to apply for an assistant principal position at another school within the district. Mr. Green's responsibilities include student discipline, staff development, and community outreach. Like the other participants, he hopes to be a principal in the near future.

David Main attended one of the most recognized preparatory high schools in the city. After completing high school he studied at a predominantly European American university, where he acquired his teacher preparation. Upon graduating from the university, Mr. Main applied for teaching positions in several suburban districts. He eventually took a position with one of the most prestigious suburban districts. After 2 years of teaching he completed his master's degree in school administration. Although Mr. Main characterized himself as an excellent teacher, his ultimate goal was to be a school administrator. Therefore, after 3 years of teaching he made the decision to leave the classroom. He interviewed in another suburban district for an assistant principal position at the high school level. Mr. Main was offered the position, which he has held for 2 years. He believes the principal at his high school has become his mentor.

The female assistant principal, *Maxine Boyd*, grew up in the rural South and attended mostly segregated schools. She never had a white teacher until she entered college. She believed that African American teachers were important for her success and attributed her aspiration to be a teacher to their support. She attended a historically Black college, where she received her baccalaureate degree in teaching. Upon graduation, she taught for 2 years in a rural community but became weary of teaching in a poverty-stricken area. She followed her family members to this city as part of the northern "Black migration." She obtained a teaching position in the city schools and ascended through the ranks to become an administrator. When the city implemented a policy that all administrators had to reside within the city limits (she did not), Ms. Boyd took a position in the suburban schools after 25 years of working in urban schools. She accepted a high school assistant principal position with a highly recognized suburban district. At the time of this study, Ms. Boyd had been in this position for 3 years. In her current administrative position, she spends most of her time with the "deseg" children who transferred to her district from the city schools. Ms. Boyd struggled with how other administrators perceived her. She believed that there was an expectation that she was responsible for the African American students in her school. While she enjoyed her role in the school, she often became tired of the stereotypes that confronted her on a daily basis. Of all of the participants, she was the most definite about the strains of feeling "out of place," yet needing to be there for the African American students.

6

DIVERSITY SELF-EFFICACY: CONCLUDING THOUGHTS

On the basis of our findings discussed in previous chapters, we offer some concluding thoughts on diversity self-efficacy and its implications for leaders to address intergroup differences. The results of the findings discussed in preceding chapters (4 and 5) suggest that principals play an important role in responding to intergroup conflict between students of color and European American school participants. Principals must examine their leadership in how they respond to issues of diversity and react to intergroup conflicts. Leadership in managing issues of diversity requires that the principals create trust, establish teams that dispel stereotypical roles for students of color, and promote dialogue on pedagogical differences in responding to students of color. We believe that in order to address intergroup differences, leaders must feel comfortable with their own beliefs and how they interact with others who are racially and ethnically different from them. The following section examines the leaders' role in addressing intergroup differences and its implications for diversity self-efficacy.

Diversity Self-Efficacy as a Leadership Necessity

The diversity challenge for leaders is to facilitate a work environment that allows and encourages an appreciation for diverse individual characteristics and dimensions. One of the struggles that leaders face in responding to intergroup conflict is how to address serious overt and subtle discrimination that occurs in the workplace (Combs, 2002). Administrators need to feel confident in their ability to acquire diversity leadership skills and to use them effectively in addressing racial overtones. The European American principals in our study noted that they had had limited exposure to people of color, expressed discomfort in addressing issues of diversity, and articulated their lack of skills in dealing with issues of race.

Interestingly, these European American principals were selected to participate in this study because they were recognized by their peers for being "socially just." Yet they relied on affective responses to issues of diversity rather than using their leadership skills to create inclusive school environments. Consequently, while leaders may have an empathetic understanding of diversity issues, they may not have the necessary theoretical grounding and practical skills that will allow them to effectively identify and deal with issues involving race in their schools. Thus, it is important to empower leaders who believe in diversity and welcome diversity challenges by providing the appropriate resources for them to master and leadership skills to model, in order to reduce intergroup conflict and promote the cultural identity of individuals in the workplace.

Pertinent leadership issues involve understanding the motivational needs and values of diverse work groups, communication practices between and among ethnic groups, and determination of expectations for authority in an organization (Chemers, Oskamp, & Costanzo, 1995). The leadership challenge in addressing diversity issues is often complicated by the leaders' exposure to others who are different from them and their discomfort in addressing racial concerns. Diversity training for leaders cannot just focus on "awareness" of the need for diversity; it must strengthen leaders in their belief that they have the capabilities to be active diversity change agents.

Diversity self-efficacy involves becoming aware of one's own beliefs about issues of diversity, which can then translate into confident modeling of positive diversity change for others and having the vision to establish an inclusive organization (Combs, 2002). Leaders have to initiate the diversity effort; they may need to jump-start it; they have to model it, organize it, tend it, guide it, sustain it, and persevere in it to motivate and encourage each individual to work effectively with others to improve organizational outcomes and effectiveness. They also have to know what they are doing. Therefore, diversity self-efficacy becomes a mechanism to assist leaders in acquiring the confidence to facilitate appropriate responses to diversity issues.

For leaders to be effective in doing all it takes, they must perceive themselves as being capable of regulating and directing their own actions regarding diversity. They must project a high level of confidence in their management capabilities to lead on issues of diversity (Combs, 2002). Leaders need personal determination and confidence to improve attitudes toward diversity and to create an inclusive environment.

If it is agreed that administrators need to develop a set of necessary skills to lead diverse work groups, diversity self-efficacy training may become an important way to evaluate leaders' performance in these contexts. Thus, diversity self-efficacy provides opportunities for the enhancement of skills and confidence to successfully navigate the challenges of diversity. To impact an individual's capacity to understand the implications of group and social identities within the workplace, there should be opportunities to practice, and to identify and rectify mistakes in, leading a diverse work force. Therefore, verbal or social persuasion techniques would transfer back to the workplace. In response to issues of diversity, leaders must go beyond managing diversity, to exercising leadership that is task specific, broad based, and diffused (Combs, 2002). If leaders can maximize their diversity self-efficacy, they can handle volatile diversity situations at the lowest level.

Through diversity self-efficacy, leaders can self-evaluate and regulate their responses to persons from different backgrounds and diversity-related situations. In this regard, performance monitoring becomes a function of the leaders' self-efficacy mechanism rather than an imposed monitoring. This context suggests that leadership in diversity management must realize the leader's comfort level, determination, and perseverance in being able to respond to areas of diversity. This bolstering of leaders' self-efficacy and application of self-efficacy beliefs may play a critical role in ensuring the transfer of skills to create an inclusive work environment.

Research reveals that when leaders are given the skills and confidence to respond to issues of diversity, they will close the gap between diversity training and diversity performance. Organizations need to provide a new focus on diversity that is about changing the workplace and not just about creating awareness of diversity-related issues. Thus, diversity self-efficacy must focus on preparing leaders by providing them with the skills to affect individual judgments and to influence change in themselves and others in the workplace.

Conclusion

Our primary objective was to examine how leaders perceive intergroup difference and its impact in creating an inclusive and responsive school environment for all children. School leaders must appreciate the importance of understanding the relationship between cultural identity and intergroup conflict as a way to build consensus among identity and organizational groups. Leaders must also develop the skills to address racial overtones and discriminatory practices. If school administrators do not have a sense of diversity self-efficacy, they will not be able to develop the capacity to regulate and direct their leadership skills on diversity-related matters. Leaders must have a clear understanding of leadership models that might be integrated into their practices to address cultural differences and intergroup conflicts that arise in diverse contexts.

Our discussion highlights critical concerns that confront leaders as they seek to create inclusive school cultures. Leaders must understand the complex dynamics that must be negotiated as they seek to respond to the divergent needs of their various constituents. As schools seek ways to respond to students, leaders need to embrace communities of difference where both minority and majority groups can be nurtured and flourish. Given the complexity of this challenge, we hope readers will reflect on the research presented here and be willing to envision a new direction in how leaders will address race in creating inclusive schools.

Emerging literature on global leadership implies that leaders can no longer focus on task and organizational goals only (Chen & Van Velsor, 1996). In motivating a diverse group of followers, leaders must build one-on-one leader–member relationships in which they create and facilitate new meaning out of diverse viewpoints. Therefore, we need to identify leaders who can tolerate ambiguity among the group identities, develop inclusive skills, and produce cultural sensitivity and a global mind-set. Leadership in dealing with intergroup conflict indicates the use of positional power to reduce tensions between organizational and individual groups. The use of positional power is necessary because leaders have the authority to influence the values, ideologies, and assumptions of the culture (Ragins, 1995).

A leadership model that responds to a diverse work force promotes the importance of building trust on issues of diversity and, through the development of personal relationships, a dialogue on cultural differences. Leadership and organizational change are viewed as important determinants in creating an inclusive organization. Chemers's research outlined three pervasive leadership functions as important in leading followers on areas of diversity. He believes that critical functions of leadership are image management, relationship development, and team coordination in confronting intergroup conflict among and between organizational participants (Chemers & Murphy, 1995). Image management refers to those aspects that affect the perception of the leader by others. Relationship development encompasses the leaders' efforts to establish an exchange that directs followers' efforts into productive channels. Thus, team coordination and deployment are concerned with how leaders create an inclusive organization to accomplish their goals.

Chemers's (1993) critical functions of effective leadership are viewed as important in diminishing stereotypes and reducing their impact on organizational functions. Leadership efforts must emphasize the importance of recognizing differences between people so that leaders can find commonality with the followers' values and abilities. This is critical because leaders must establish credibility and trust as a way to lead a diverse group of teachers. Trust levels often differ among cross-gender and cross-race dyads in dealing with identity groups (Scott, 1983). Intergroup conflicts in areas of cultural differences and group boundaries in these schools might have been alleviated if leaders had gained the trust of all of the teachers.

Developing relationships between the leader and followers is a major determinant for coaching and guiding both minority and majority group members (Chemers & Murphy, 1995). Bass (1985) believes that leaders dealing with group conflict must practice "individualized consideration" in which they attempt to maximize personal growth for minority members. Because of intergroup conflict surrounding cultural differences, minority members need to perceive leaders as fair and having a sense of equity. Additionally, leaders have to understand that people with different cultural identities in the workplace perceive differently how their work is validated. Thus, leaders need to understand that in establishing personal relationships with their diverse followers, they must also recognize differences in motivating their followers (Jones, 2002).

Leaders who are effective in dealing with intergroup conflict must also consider team coordination and deployment (Chemers & Murphy, 1995). As a result of intergroup conflict in areas of incongruent goals and group boundaries, minority members feel that the leader must develop teams that will allow them opportunities to be successful. Both majority and minorities must have similar work/task behaviors that create a collectivist-cooperative approach. Problems of microinequities of majority groups result in the exclusion of informal peer support, networking, and mentoring as a way to support minorities (Rowe, 1991). Ultimately, leaders play an important role in defining employee behaviors and the way minority groups are perceived as qualified and accepted in the organizational culture (Ragins, 1995). Leadership in managing issues of diversity requires that the leaders create trust, establish teams that dispel stereotypical roles for students of color, and promote dialogue on pedagogical differences in responding to learning needs of students of color.

PART III

LEADERSHIP USING A STRATEGIC PROCESS

Given the reality of a diverse population in schools, attention should be paid to how schools can promote social norms for cohesiveness and mutual understanding. In creating such settings, differences between people are explained as plausible and valid alternative customs, traditions, and points of view. In such a scenario, participants support each other as they begin to understand and appreciate the validation of alternative points of view, and establish social norms that allow them to become interdependent. This interdependence creates the processes by which people form the social norms that facilitate positive working conditions. Thus, inclusiveness is derived from a supportive environment that affirms diversity as an explicit value. The chapters in part III deal with two important areas: how to address issues of diversity in schools based on the leadership competencies we have developed, and how to develop a strategic process using an integrative plan that will assist in improving student outcomes. We believe that schools can create positive workplace relationships for all school participants by using the information presented in these chapters.

Leadership Competencies

While in previous chapters we have provided information on intergroup differences and the role of the school administrator in addressing these differences, in chapter 7 we develop the framework for leadership competencies essential to leading in diverse contexts. The ability to address intergroup conflicts is an important skill if a leader is to create inclusive contexts. Leaders who have a good understanding of their own ethnicity and its implications for interactions with others will, be better able to create an adaptive organization for diverse participants, prevent their differences from being used against them, and leverage difference to create a richer environment for the school.

We use Lewis's (2003) research that examines how people construct and negotiate racial identity in schools. She indicates that a racial ascription process takes place as individuals socially categorize differences, establish racial boundaries, and identify inclusive or exclusionary power practices. What comes of this can present challenges that leaders must confront, through their understanding of how racial boundaries are formed in schools, to ensure that a racialization process shapes how children and school participants perceive race in an affirming way. School leaders also need to understand how the school context creates coded places where certain rules and structural and cultural repertoires have implications for how students of color will be educated. From this perspective, leaders in diverse contexts must become cultural integrators and consensus builders who acquire an understanding of their constituents' backgrounds and perspectives and establish leader–member trust (Dovido, Gaertner, & Bachman, 2001).

Leaders need to have some sense of organizational direction and a willingness to revisit how their school's image is viewed by parents and community on diversity-related issues. In response to diversity, leaders must establish a relational identity orientation so that the school's culture respects the cultural identities of its members. Last, the way administrators structure their schools to improve student outcomes requires them to examine their personnel practices, how they establish team structures to support teachers, and the induction programs to socialize teachers for these contexts.

Concomitant with a sense of direction is the leader's sense of organizational identity. This means that the leader must clearly define how he or she is going to identify personnel who can work with these diverse students, structure the organization to ensure that all students' needs are met, and establish an identity orientation that creates dense and integrated networks. In addition, leaders need to understand how both school participants and the public perceive the school's responsiveness to issues of diversity. Organizational identity theories focus on the interactions between individuals within an organization that establish salient beliefs about the participants' uniqueness (Albert & Whetten, 1985). Organizational image is the public's perception of a given organization based on its actions and achievements (Fombrun, 1996). These theories suggest that when a leader does not understand the interdependence between organizational identity and image, a school will not be viewed as meeting the needs of diverse student participants. From this perspective, leaders need to focus on strategies and actions that support a school identity and image that reflect the school's diverse constituents' interests.

Leading in a diverse context requires that the administrator be able to create a climate of interpersonal cooperation, establish relational partners, and foster an "other-oriented" motivation. Theories of identity orientation examine the manner in which organizations create particular contextual features that support individual and/or collective identities of members. Brickson's model (2000) suggests that leaders who take a relational approach to identity orientation are likely to include the diverse backgrounds and perspectives of school participants to create an inclusive school. Leaders must facilitate interpersonal cooperation among and between groups and support the unique backgrounds, characteristics, and skills of teachers, students, and community members. According to this theory, schools activating a relationship identity orientation will produce better organizational outcomes and improve attitudes about diversity.

The final leadership competency that we consider is the power and commitment to restructure the school organization to ensure that all participants' needs are addressed. Leaders need to create an adaptive organizational structure so that the school will keep pace as its diverse makeup changes over time. Chemers (1993) has provided a basis for interpreting how the effective management of diversity is essential to effective leadership. Team coordination and deployment focus on the leader's ability to use his or her talents to effectively engage the talents of all participants in accomplishing organizational objectives (Chemers & Murphy, 1995). The leader focuses on accomplishing organizational goals by providing workers with the necessary resources. Emphasis on team formation and induction programs will assist in attracting and retaining a diverse work force. In addition, leaders spend considerable energy socializing teachers to these diverse contexts, supporting teachers from their entry phase into their growth and success phases.

Developing a Strategic Process to Enhance Student Outcomes

The leader's ability to develop an adaptive organizational structure for schools with diverse populations is a major component in ensuring that all students are provided with the means to be successful. Leaders must deal with the paradox of adaptation, where the tensions of the traditional structure often collide with an adherence to implementing participatory principles (Nicoteria, Clinkscales, & Walker, 2003). Districts dictate rules and structures that result in control, hierarchy, and authority. Tensions exist when there are restrictive rules that dictate the nature of democracy. So the question that needs to be examined is, Is there a structural process that schools might use to address issues of enhancing diversity?

In chapter 8 we review the organizational literature to determine how corporations have dealt with diversity and the implications for changing corporate structure, hiring diverse personnel, and improving organizational effectiveness. Most of that literature has focused on the development of a strategic process to improve organizational effectiveness and create positive outcomes in diversity-related issues. Reasoning that if schools have a strategic process to redesign their organizational system, we can better address issues of student outcomes and organizational effectiveness, we reconfigured how corporate plans might be shaped and applied to a school context.

At present, we have worked with a handful of both urban and suburban schools and with several school practitioners to assist us in defining what a strategic diversity process needs to consider when implemented in a school context. While we do not profess to have all the answers to what a strategic diversity plan should include, we contend that the strategic process affords some useful options and considerations. One must remember that most school cultures in the United States were established when a majority of teachers were white and instructional practices and curriculum goals were quite homogeneous. Therefore, for schools to develop a strategic process, they need to critically examine the district's philosophy surrounding issues of diversity. Each school must determine whether present policies hinder or support its organizational goal to be, and to be recognized as, an inclusive school.

To begin the process of implementing a diversity plan, we recommend that schools complete a "culture" audit much like what Thomas (1991) suggests for organizations that are undergoing a strategic diversity process. A school should examine its hiring practices in terms of whether it seeks and retains a diverse teaching force, look at the disaggregation of student outcomes (achievement scores; discipline referrals; high school graduation rates; percentage of students of color in gifted and advanced placement [AP] classes; and so forth), and analyze how the school is organized to address diversity-related issues. This process will provide a glimpse of how the school deals with contradictory structures through an examination of present policies that influence student outcomes and establish an exclusive climate.

After reviewing the "culture audit" data, a school must identify the assumptions that are prevalent in the school and determine how the school participants can work collaboratively to develop a systematic process to address issues of diversity. Reviewing the culture audit identifies the assumptions that are prevalent in the school's culture and determines a strategic process to address how diversity is implemented and integrated into the culture of the school. The next phase is to implement and integrate the plan into the overall school improvement model. The final phase is to establish ongoing evaluation of the plan so there will be continuous monitoring of progress and the development of benchmarks that clearly demonstrate that the strategic process is successfully addressing issues of diversity.

In chapter 8 we strongly suggest that in implementing a strategic diversity plan, schools consider all the dimensions of diversity if they are to integrate a diversity plan into the school. While the strategic diversity plan spells out a clear process, its actual implementation can be quite complex. Schools that complete the culture audit must move from just talking about what the audit implies to what they can do to change the school context. Research on how corporations implement their strategic process, from completing the culture audit to putting the plan into operation, shows this to be the most difficult step (Thomas, 1991; Cox, 2001).

After reviewing the literature on the possibility of using a strategic process, we cautiously assert that if schools just complete the diversity plan, organizational effectiveness will improve. As researchers, we believe that the implementation and integration of a diversity plan is a possible solution. But we do not propose that schools and districts see it as the only method for addressing issues of diversity. Hence, we also suggest in chapter 8 that schools consider that when addressing issues of diversity, one must realize that diversity matters elicit emotionally-laden discussions among school participants. The leadership needs to possess a degree of expertise about diversity issues that extends well beyond basic administrative issues of hiring and retention. Task forces must be integrated and reflect not only the teachers' ethnicity but that of other school participants as well.

Corporations that have developed a diversity strategy have increased their organizational flexibility, retained and improved the quality of their personnel, and improved their organizational outcomes (Cox, 2001). If schools are to be successful in managing diversity, will a strategic process be a possible solution? Schools that are responding to external constraints based on their students' ethnic composition and internal accountability demands from policy makers may benefit from developing a strategic diversity process. However, such a process must be developed in the context of a school's goals and values, and in response to its internal and external concerns. Therefore, Chapter 8 provides an overview of why strategic plans are important, and we present a diversity plan we consider appropriate for schools.

7

LEADERSHIP IN DIVERSE CONTEXTS: TOWARD A THEORETICAL FRAMEWORK

Introduction

Current immigration trends are resulting in increasing racial and ethnic diversity in the United States. Cox (1994) and Brislin (1990) suggest that recent generations of immigrants, refugees, and racial minorities are less willing to accept the "melting pot" ideology than earlier groups. As a result of these demographic shifts, racial and ethnic minorities are increasingly vocal in their demands for respect of their cultures and cultural identities (Thomas, 1996). Therefore, an assimilationalist view of ethnicity in which racial-ethnic minorities are expected to embrace mainstream culture and reject their own is increasingly problematic (Gudykunst, 1991).

A pluralist perspective suggests that ethnicity is an internal attribute that promotes the acceptance of ethnic identification. However, due to the majority group's limited exposure, many still feel uncomfortable interacting with people who are culturally or racially different from them. Furthermore, majority members feel an even greater uneasiness when minority group members choose to assert their culture rather than assimilate. Given the importance of diversity in organizations and the present trend to employ an increasingly diverse work force, there is a need to develop a leadership frame that will help administrators to reflect on their practices when working in diverse contexts.

What are the linkages between diversity and leadership, and how do these relationships influence the way leaders operate within their organizations to establish amicable interactions among their diverse employees? In this chapter, we provide insights into important implications for leadership within diverse contexts as reflected in the current diversity literature, and we propose a framework of leadership theories that practitioners may use to enhance their leadership effectiveness in diverse school contexts.

Diversity and Leadership

There is a paucity of research that specifically addresses leadership in situations of diversity except in terms of undertaking efforts to make organizations more tolerant or accepting of differences (DiTomaso & Hooijberg, 1996). Much is written about the leader's "color-blindness," in which he or she sees workers as the same and implicitly as white. Inherent in the leader's expectation is the notion that minority workers will assimilate into the organization's dominant culture (Dovido, Gaertner, & Bachman, 2001). Diversity perspectives pose challenges to many such beliefs in organization and management.

Chen and VanVelsor (1996) argue that diversity leadership research and practice must consider multiple aspects in order to effectively address the needs of a diverse work force. Their critique of mainstream leadership theories observes that while these theories focus on interpersonal and intrapersonal leadership skills as cultivated in a traditionally homogeneous environment, they neglect crucial intergroup dimensions of leadership. By defining leadership in terms of personality characteristics and how leaders use their abilities to influence their employees, mainstream leadership theories are unable to look beyond the usual organizationally (and homogeneously) defined relationships with followers, to how a leader is impacted by and influences others' cultural identities (Chen & Van Velsor, 1996). The current focus of mainstream leadership theories is still the rational, purposeful, and goal-oriented leadership processes (Chemers & Murphy, 1995), with their explicit basis in a homogeneous or strongly dominant-culture orientation.

Diversity research emphasizes group identities and views them as cultural identities. The concept of cultural identities serves as a psychological lens to examine the impact of diversity at the individual level and its implications for group interactions (Chen & Van Velsor, 1996). This understanding of this intercultural perspective emphasizes the idea that we are all cultural beings, shaped and oriented by the cultures of the groups to which we belong (Ferdman, 1995). Thus, leaders need to understand cultural differences among groups and their implications for interpersonal and organizational outcomes and processes.

We contend that leadership skills should include not only interpersonal skills in responding to issues of diversity but also a competent understanding of the importance of culture and group identities. Unlike mainstream leadership theories, diversity leadership research examines how social, racial, and cultural issues that originate outside the organization have implications for leader–member exchanges. Diversity research examines how race and gender affect organizational networks, career opportunities for people of color, mentoring relationships, group dynamics, and communication styles (Chemers et al., 1995; Chen & Van Velsor, 1996; Ragins, 1995; Livers & Carver, 2003; Cox, 2001). Therefore, leaders who work with members of different ethnic backgrounds need to recognize cultural differences in their followers and understand how these differences may affect the ways in which relationships among followers are developed and negotiated.

Chen and Van Velsor (1996) believe there should be new directions for research and practice in diversity leadership. In their review, researchers place more emphasis on the "other," so the focus of leadership is not on task completion but on ways to create an interdependence between the various cultural groups. Additionally, DiTomaso and Hooijberg (1996) state that just asking leaders to understand the context of various subcultures and group processes may contribute to misunderstanding and miscommunication among groups. Thus, in order to enhance organizational performance, leaders must remake the relationships of people in various categories to ensure equal power and opportunity. They must act as role models to create bridges and safe pathways for those who have been hindered from participating to their full capacity. Finally, leaders must provide a space for all followers to learn and develop their own commitment to diversity, and they must have zero tolerance for discriminatory behavior (DiTomaso & Hooijberg, 1996).

Leadership Skills to Address Intergroup Differences

Given that there is limited research on which leadership models are most appropriate for addressing issues of diversity, administrators often struggle with their leadership decisions in diverse contexts. Therefore, we have identified a few leadership theories that we believe frame how leaders can respond to their diverse followers. The models we present are integrated conceptions responding to the crucial need for leaders to address their biases in relation to their ethnically diverse work force, develop a more follower-oriented relationship, and create a cognitive component for self-monitoring and efficacy.

In this section, we have selected several theoretical models that are relevant for creating an inclusive school. We have combined, extended, and modified them in order to examine the dynamics of cultural identities in the workplace and to understand the impact of intergroup relationships among and between majority and ethnically diverse members of the work force. On the basis of our previous and current research, we have identified four leadership behaviors we believe are important for diverse contexts. We believe that these leadership skills are not isolated qualities but are interdependent and mediated in leaders' administrative practices. Thus, leadership in a diverse context is framed by the interchange between leader and follower and is dependent on the following variables: (1) a leader's capacity to understand his or her own cultural identity and its influence on interactions with others who are racially and ethnically different from him or her; (2) a leader's capacity to create an organizational direction that responds to how the school is perceived by its diverse constituency; (3) a leader's ability to implement a relational identity orientation in order to promote interpersonal cooperation and create dense and integrated networks among and between school participants; and (4) a leader's ability to establish an organizational structure that adapts to the changing needs of diverse students and teacher participants. In the ensuing discussion we will address the significance of these leadership skills and their interdependence in creating inclusive schools.

Understanding and Challenging Racial Boundaries

One can argue that in leading a diverse group of followers and constituencies, leaders must be knowledgeable about participants' ethnic and cultural differences. According to Chen and Van Velsor (1996), the bicultural identity of people of color is often an undervalued strength within the organization. Several studies reveal that a bicultural leadership becomes critical when responding to issues of diversity in the workplace. Parker and Ogilvie (1996) believe that African American women's experiences in the workplace reveal the importance of culture-specific models that may produce strategic responses to emulate. Bell (1990) contends that career-oriented African American women live on the boundaries of two distinctly different cultures and are able to reshape interactional contexts constrained by race and gender bias.

Additionally, Madsen and Mabokela's (2002) research on African American principals in suburban desegregated schools demonstrates that one's ethnicity is important in addressing intercultural contact among groups and navigating between two cultures. Without losing their cultural identity, these leaders were cultural integrators and consensus builders who had acquired a great deal of understanding about the diversity of groups. Thus, as a result of their intercultural ability, they were able to establish leader–member trust. The important issue here is whether, because of their ethnic backgrounds or leadership capabilities, leaders of color are critical in heading heterogeneous groups.

We contend that a leader's ethnicity has implications for how he or she will address issues of diversity and also for how he or she will perceive his or her own cultural identity in relation to those of followers and constituencies. The concept of cultural identity is defined as the person's individual image of the cultural features that characterize his or her group(s) and the reflection of these features in his or her self-representation. Cultural identity is proposed as a concept that represents the individual-level reflection of culture as it is constructed by each individual (Ferdman, 1995). Cultural identity addresses our sense of ourselves as cultural beings and guides an individual's behavior. Cultural identity differs from social identity in that it focuses on the inside boundary of what the individual perceives to be the behavioral and attitudinal bases or consequences of the in-group and out-group categories.

The authors believe that if leaders are to create a relational identity orientation in the workplace, they need to understand the cultural identity of all participants. Thus, leaders need to ensure that in diverse contexts all group members are seen as unique individuals with social identity characteristics (Brickson, 2000). Additionally, leaders must ensure that all participants perceive themselves as integrated and valued organization members. The authors believe that the attention to cultural identity allows leaders to understand systematic variations in how people see themselves as connected to their group(s) and serves to examine how diversity at the individual level affects group-level differences (Ferdman, 1995). Also, as leaders attempt to envision their own cultural identity in order to ensure a common group identity in the organization, they must not ask participants to forsake their subgroup identities. Finally, leaders must simultaneously recognize the importance of cultural identity in creating a balance for generalizable intergroup attitudes (Dovido et al., 2001) (See Appendix C).

Through the understanding of cultural identity, leaders can understand the intercultural connections between them and other ethnic groups in diverse contexts. Lewis (2003) notes that in understanding racial identification, we see markers of difference and then make choices about how we assign an identity to others. As a result, leaders need to understand racial boundary formation (the establishment of boundaries between racial categories is simultaneously created or reinforced) and its implications for acts of inclusion or exclusion (Lewis, 2003). From this, leaders must understand how schools become racially coded and the racial overtones in the ways rules and structures are influenced by power. To go forward, how can leaders create schools where children envision race and see others who are ethnically different from them, and help children think about racial identities in school contexts (Lewis, 2003)? The final aspect for the leader is to not only understand the importance of racial boundaries, but also to be willing to challenge the systemic and institutional biases of schools so that all feel included (see appendix C).

In understanding and challenging racial boundaries, the leader needs to be a relationship builder in order to ensure similar interests among groups and a connectedness. Leaders must believe that all contribute to the greater good, so they envision creative outlets for people to explore their own cultural identities in relation to "others." They promote the view that everyone is a part of the whole. Therefore, when some participants struggle to understand the complexity of cultural identity using a "color-blind" approach, leaders address out-group bias so they can create more positive intergroup relations. In this way, such a leadership approach becomes an effective strategy that facilitates an empathetic arousal so that there is an "other" motivation. In understanding and challenging racial boundaries, the leader needs to reduce competition and establish a common identity so that all are working toward collective goals (Dovido et al., 2001).

Another aspect to understanding and challenging racial boundaries is that the leader must be community oriented. If leaders are to be responsive to constituencies outside the school context, they must create an environment for community involvement. Leaders who are cultural integrators make community members feel valued and part of the school's identity. If leaders can harness the energy of community participants to their potential, then the school will benefit from their commitment. Finally, to be community oriented, leaders must ensure that no one person or group can be the sole voice. Leaders have to share the power to integrate multiple leadership skills into their community.

The leadership skill of understanding and challenging racial boundaries becomes important in acknowledging not only one's own cultural identity but also how the interactions of multiple group identities are racially categorized in these contexts. Leaders have the capacity to prevent schools from being racially categorized, so that schools can become inclusive places. However, if leaders do not understand the complexity of cultural identity, then they will not be able to challenge how schools go about creating inequities. Furthermore, leaders must be relationship builders in order to establish linkages between schools and community groups. If the parents perceive that the school leader is willing to challenge boundaries for students of color, there will be a sense of community and parent involvement (see appendix C).

Creating an Organizational Identity and Responsive School Image

Leaders have to understand how to create an organizational identity in which the school's image is perceived as inclusive. In response to this image perception, leaders need to develop an organizational identity that promotes a responsive environment. Thus, leaders promote an organizational direction that will change the school organization and ensure that school participants will be responsive to its diverse constituency. We believe leaders must have a strong sense of organizational direction as a way to enhance how the school is perceived by school participants in terms of diversity-related issues. It is important for leaders to understand that their schools must establish an internal identity. This identity affects how exchanges will be perceived among school participants and how an image will be projected to community members and stakeholders. Responsiveness to diversity has become increasingly relevant for leaders interested in understanding how they influence and maintain organizational identity and a school image in working with a diverse group of participants (see appendix C).

Using these definitions, we applied organizational identity and image theory to explore how leaders perceive the interactions among their actions, organizational identity, and image in addressing issues of diversity. A lack of understanding by the leader regarding the interdependence between organizational identity and image may result in organizational instability. Hence, leaders must clearly understand that their role is to create an adaptive instability such that the interpretation of an organization's projected image by outsiders must result in a responsive examination of identity (Gioa, Schultz, & Corley, 2000).

Organizational identity is defined as the organization members' collective understanding of the features that are presumed to be central and permanent and that distinguish the organization from other organizations (Albert & Whetten, 1985). A school reflects its organizational identity through its core beliefs. Yet, when the community demographics shift, what does that mean to its present population and its ability to reorganize in accordance with its changing, diverse constituency? A school's organizational identity becomes its expressed values, but these values are not always fixed or stable. Even though an organization's core values and mission remain, the actions of the school population may take different forms over time. So, as organizations and their constituencies become more ethnically diverse, leaders have to create an organizational identity that ensures that it addresses the complexity of diversity.

Organizational identity is constructed not only through the interactions of individuals within the organization but also in interactions with outsiders such as community members. Thus, an organization's identity is embedded in its individuals and is a social construction based on repeated interactions with others (Cooley, 1902). Therefore, an organization's identity emerges from the process of interaction and is sustained by a social construction of repeated interactions with others. As diverse members enter the school doors, they bring with them their socially constructed realities of what they believe is the purpose of schooling. Therefore, when school members interact, there is a continual need to reconfigure the organizational direction so as to ensure that there is a collective mission for all students.

Organizational image is based on how the organization's members believe outsiders view the organization. This orientation implies that an organization wants to project an image that is based on its organizational identity. Thus, an organizational identity projects a desired future image that communicates a vision to both insiders and outsiders, a vision to be achieved (Cooley, 1902). A projected image conveys a socially desirable, managed impression that emphasizes selected aspects of identity; it can even conceal or misrepresent identity. Thus, organizational image can be construed as an internal conception whose perception focuses on an insider perspective (Berstein, 1984). Organizational image can also take on an external approach by focusing on perceptions held by outsiders.

The public's perception or impression of how a school meets the needs of its diverse population makes organizational image an important consideration. A community's or parents' perception of a school is a transient impression, a collective judgment based on the actions the school takes and its achievements. Thus, a school's reputation can be distinguished from that of other schools by how equitably it treats its students and parents. If we are to be responsive to our changing student demographics, then leaders need to understand how a school's image determines the degree of parent and community involvement.

Identity and image interrelationships become the catalyst for the way organizations examine their organizational direction on diversity-related issues. When a school's image is inconsistent with its constituency, a destabilizing dynamic results. Thus, schools need to reconstruct their sense of self; they need to rethink who they are in order to create a positive image (Gioa et al., 2000). School members need to keep receiving feedback from outsiders in order to remain sensitive to the views held by the community and parents. When a school is perceived negatively by a sector of the community, a disconnect of an implicit or explicit comparison between identity and external image occurs. Thus, the concept of adaptive instability becomes a consequence of the relationship between a school's image and its organizational identity. When a school's image and its organizational identity are not aligned, there will be a disconnect between the school participants and the community members.

When this instability between organizational identity and image occurs, schools need to adapt to the demands of their diverse student population. This reciprocal process of projection and modification results in an examination of a school's identity. Therefore, schools must establish an organizational identity that promotes an image of being responsive to issues of diversity. Leaders in diverse contexts need to understand how traditional organizational values create an organizational identity. As schools' demographics change, leaders need to adapt to participants' perceptions of how their organization responds to its participants. If schools are to be inclusive, then leaders must make efforts to implement necessary organizational changes, so parents and community members feel secure that their school will help their children achieve.

Developing a Relational Identity Orientation Leadership

Although multiple approaches are used to understand the impact of diversity on organizational effectiveness, most researchers agree that the identification process plays a central role in ensuring positive effects of diversity in the workplace. Our review of diversity literature reveals that leaders need to understand the importance of the cultural identities of their followers. The literature also calls for leaders to be able to facilitate an identity orientation that promotes a relational perspective in which leaders have frequent and quality interactions with coworkers. Thus, we believe that another skill that leaders must have is the ability to establish a relational identity orientation in the workplace in order to promote positive exchanges among followers and constituencies (see appendix C).

Based on Brewer's (1991) identification processes work, Brickson (2000) believes that each identity orientation is associated with a primary motivation among individuals. Also, she believes that one's identity orientation is related to the type of self-knowledge about one's own traits and characteristics, one's roles in relation to others, and one's group's prototypes. Thus, this sense of self-knowledge will have implications for how a person will work with others who may be ethnically different from him or her. While the specific work orientation determines personal relationships between individuals, that orientation is activated by the contextualization of the organization and its structure. These organizational features include both organizational structure and task and reward structure. How leaders understand the importance of identity orientation and its relationship to how they facilitate both identity and organizational groups will impact organizational outcomes. Thus, if we are to address issues of diversity, there are two considerations: the leader needs first to understand how participants will interact with others who are different from them and, second, to structure the school to support these differences through its personnel practices, teaming, and socialization and induction programs.

Brickson's (2000) identity orientation model illustrates the relationship among formal context, identity orientation activation, and individual and organizational outcomes. These three identity orientations are personal, relational, and collective. Brickson believes that by responding to identity orientations in the workplace, the mode of organization will create an environment that fosters one kind of orientation and plays down other orientations in demographically diverse settings. Personal identity orientation emerges when the organization establishes an individualistic rather than an integrative work environment. This context produces an environment in which people are rewarded individually and facilitates a competitive experience. Workers create zero-sum outcomes in which they care only about their own welfare, advance their own positions, and are not motivated to help others. Thus, a personal identity orientation becomes problematic because it promotes a perception that the system is just, creates ambivalence toward minorities, and establishes a competitive environment.

In contrast, a collective identity orientation establishes a static and salient group membership. While the organization is less structured, more group integration occurs. Individuals within this organizational structure view themselves based on their group membership. Kanter (1977) believes that segmentalist organizations in which individuals are grouped on the basis of categories such as men and women, or minority and majority, results in group boundaries. As a result, performance is measured and rewarded according to group membership, and the motivation for individuals is to support one's own group (Kanter, 1977). Demographic distinctions may activate a collective identity in which stereotypes about minorities may affect organizational effectiveness, resulting in intergroup conflicts (Brickson, 2000). A collectivist categorization process that supports only one specific group will impact workplace relations and create in-group and out-group conflicts. Often this collectivist perspective results in minorities experiencing low self-esteem and in a lack of organizational integration (Brewer & Miller, 1984).

Brickson (2000) believes that when a leader creates a relational orientation, individuals are motivated to ensure the benefit of others. Thus, the organizational structure promotes interpersonal cooperation, and groups of individuals are not the focus. This orientation emphasizes integrated networks and relationships in which there are positive interactions and group differences are not encouraged. Leaders who create a relational identity orientation help individuals see themselves as partners in unique relationships; such individuals are more likely to cooperate. To achieve this, leaders break group tasks into dyadic structures and rotate the group's composition to increase the interpersonal attachments. Because of the greater likelihood of demographically integrated group networks, minorities will perceive themselves as more integrated and feel valued for their contributions. Leaders who create a school culture that activates a relationship orientation will produce better organizational outcomes and establish optimistic viewpoints about diversity (Brewer & Miller, 1984).

Given certain factors, such as personality traits and group composition, a formal organizational context often constrains an individual's behavior. Thus it is not a question of whether, but of to what end, that behavior will be constrained. How schools define goals and expectations will determine the school participants' behavioral patterns (Kanter, 1977). Schools striving to address issues of diversity in areas of organizational structure and task and reward structure need to understand the implications of identity orientation for their organization's members (Brickson, 2000). If we want to create an inclusive school, we need to examine the importance of the identity orientation of school participants and be aware of how the school's organizational structure will impact these two aspects.

The types of skills needed to create a relational orientation for diverse workers can be located in the interpersonal-, group-, and organizational-level forces that affect the way an individual constructs an identity within a group. To create an identity orientation leadership, administrators need to examine how the school's task and reward structure shapes the nature of interpersonal- and group-level phenomena. The authors advocate that leaders establish workplace relationships that promote an "other" and create interpersonal attachments. Therefore, when a teacher enters a school and brings with him or her a self-definition as an individual and also as a member of an identity group, these attributes will affect how he or she establishes relationships with others who are different from him or her. If teachers have had very little exposure to those who are different from them, this may influence their interactions with others. Administrators have to promote an "other" focus, then create a task and reward structure in which acceptance of differences is supported.

Developing an Adaptive Organizational Structure to Address Intergroup Differences

The interdependence of addressing racial boundaries, creating an organizational direction to improve the school's image, and establishing a relational identity orientation to support a diverse work force requires the administrator to develop an adaptive organizational structure. In developing a leadership framework for diverse contexts, we contend that leaders must structure the organization so as to establish an adaptive formation that will create a teaming structure to accomplish the organizational goals effectively. In creating this structure, leaders and their followers have a sense of ownership to implement the desired strategies in order to change the structural and institutional barriers. We believe that to meet their organizational goals, administrators need a flexible arrangement that evolves and expands as the diverse participants enter the school building. Thus, we believe that leaders must create a task and reward structure that will shape how teachers of color and European American teachers will interact with each other and their constituencies to ensure organizational effectiveness (see appendix C).

We believe that Chemers's leadership effectiveness model is useful in describing how to structure an organization to address diversity issues. Chemers (1993) developed an integrative leadership model that he believes incorporates the relationship between leader actions and group outcomes as defined by situational variables. He believes that his integrative model can provide a basis for understanding how diversity issues are related to effective leadership. We used Chemers's third category, team coordination and deployment. The leader's ability to successfully coordinate the intellectual, material, and emotional resources available in the group is important for accomplishing the organizational mission.

With team employment and deployment, Chemers (1993) argues, the deployment of resources of the leader and the group will determine how the motivation and commitment of leader and followers are translated into group performance. Chemers uses the term *environment-fit* to refer to how the organization is structured. He maintains that in meeting the needs of diverse participants, the organization allows for adaptability in response to new tasks and situations. In highly structured organizations, there is a paradox of adaptation in which there is tension between traditional structure (with low adherence to participatory processes) and the need to adapt (Nicoteria, Clinkscales, & Walker, 2003). Chemers believes that organizations that are highly structured will result in a culture that is not flexible and that will detract from organizational effectiveness. If the organization is moderately structured, individuals within the organization will be more accustomed to being flexible.

Leaders must reconcile the differences between group members' perceptions and expectations, whether caused by ethnic or other factors. Leaders and followers from different ethnic groups may have differing views of how involved and hands-on their leaders should be. Leaders need to understand the importance of giving meaning to and defining the environment in order to convince followers that they have the capability to be successful. School administrators must build relationships with teachers, focusing less on tasks to be accomplished. If leaders are to create a relational identity orientation, they must support teachers so they will be able to expand their understanding of cultural differences that may underlie their instructional practices.

Another aspect of team employment and deployment is the importance of leadership and group process. Diversity has implications for group dynamics and group decisions (Chemers, 1995). When goals and procedures are clear, both heterogeneous and homogeneous teams will be successful. However, complex tasks have implications for how teams will complete them, and more diverse team composition has implications for how teams will be effective ("teaming"). Leaders need to consider how to establish team structures so that they contain an ethnically diverse group. Teams with members of different ethnic groups tend to have a more collectivist, cooperative orientation to tasks, while homogeneous (European American) teams tend to be more individualistic in completing their tasks (Cox, 1994). Given the complexity of leading in diverse contexts, it becomes apparent that how the leader structures the organization and defines team composition will impact organizational effectiveness. Leaders need to understand how diversity and the potential coordination difficulties of heterogeneous groups can be integrated into the organizational structure.

Besides the teaming aspect, leaders need to understand the individual processes inherent in the way that leveraging diversity will influence members as they negotiate communication differences, organizational roles, and their cultural identity. As noted in the first chapters of this book, the African American teachers often struggled with how to define their place in desegregated contexts. Hence, leaders need to understand the importance of what it means to recruit and retain personnel and of how they work with all teachers to differentiate between mainstream culture and one's own culture. We believe that leaders must create a socialization process for all teachers entering diverse contexts. Teachers must be supported from their entry phase into their success stage in order to ensure that all children are successful in school. Leaders play an important role in ensuring that teachers use culturally relevant and equitable practices. By teaming teachers with other successful teachers, socializing teachers for diverse contexts, and supporting teachers' cultural identities, a leader can structure the organization for diversity (see appendix C).

We believe that in responding to a diverse constituency, leaders must arrange an organizational structure that is flexible and expands as the school population shifts its demographics. Leveraging diversity aims at continuous adaptability on the organizational level and homeostasis at the participant level. In forming an adaptive structure, leaders must strike a balance between creating relationships and focusing on tasks to be accomplished. Leadership must promote participatory processes in which teams reflect heterogeneous diversity and equal power distribution. Schools must strive to correlate the ethnic composition of their faculties with that of their students in order to maintain a healthy school image. Leaders must create a socialization process for teachers' entry and adjustment phase so that they can work with a diverse constituency. Finally, leaders must facilitate a culture that supports differences, so all school participants will be able to negotiate successfully between their own culture and that of their school. The leader needs to understand how his or her personality and beliefs impact diverse contexts and the many implications of his or her role in creating inclusiveness. Leadership makes a difference in the success of groups and is critical in facilitating an organizational structure that supports a diverse work force.

Conclusion

This chapter has provided a theoretical framework that may be helpful in defining the leadership skills needed to create inclusive schools and to address intergroup differences. This theoretical framework emerged from our interviews with principals from ethnically diverse groups in high-performing multicultural schools. These principals had four leadership practices in common: (1) they understood how their own cultural identity affects their relationships with their diverse school participants; (2) they established an organizational identity that influenced how they responded to the school's image; (3) they worked hard to ensure that there was a relational identity orientation in which there were interpersonal attachments and dense and integrated networks; and (4) they created an organizational structure that was adaptive in order to develop a socialization process for all teachers entering the school. Based on our early findings, this chapter provides an overview of theoretical frames we believe are important for leaders to develop if they are to be successful in diverse contexts (see appendix C).

In summary, when leading a diverse group of teachers and students, knowledge about school participants' ethnic and cultural differences becomes imperative. Lewis's (2003) research reflects how people construct and negotiate racial identity in schools. She indicates that a racial ascription process takes place as individuals socially categorize differences, establish racial boundaries, and identify inclusive or exclusionary power practices. Related literature suggests that intercultural knowledge and experiences inform leader–member interactions regarding problem solving and decision making (Cox, 2000). From this perspective, leaders in diverse contexts must become cultural integrators and consensus builders who acquire understanding of their constituents' backgrounds and perspectives, and establish leader–member trust (Dovido et al., 2001).

Additionally, leaders need to understand the importance of having an organizational identity that develops a school image that is responsive to its diverse constituency. Therefore, organizational identity theories focus on the interactions between individuals within an organization that establish salient beliefs about the followers' uniqueness (Albert & Whetten, 1985). Organizational image is the public's perception of an organization based on its actions and achievements (Fombrun, 1996). These theories suggest that if the leader does not understand the interdependence between organizational identity and image, an organization that cannot adapt to its diverse constituency may soon find that its public image has deteriorated badly, thereby rendering the organization unstable. From this perspective, leaders need to focus on strategies and actions that support a school identity and images that reflect its diverse constituents' interests.

Leaders must create a relational identity that supports individual and group differences in schools. Brickson's model (2000) suggests that leaders who take a relational approach to identity orientation are likely to leverage the diverse backgrounds and perspectives of their school's participants to create an inclusive school. This relational approach to identity orientation suggests that leaders must facilitate interpersonal cooperation among and between groups, and support the unique backgrounds, characteristics, and skills of teachers, students, and community members. According to this theory, schools activating a relational identity orientation will produce better organizational outcomes and improve attitudes about diversity.

Finally, a leader must structure the school to support teaming and participatory practices, and develop a socialization process to support teachers in working with diverse learners. In team coordination and deployment, the leader uses his or her talents to facilitate the followers' talents so that they can accomplish the organizational objectives (Chemers & Murphy, 1995). Therefore, the leader's focus is on accomplishing the organizational goals by providing workers with the necessary resources. Teaming and induction programs are needed to assist in attracting and retaining a diverse work force to respond to issues of diversity (Orbe, 1998; Dickens & Dickens, 1991).

STRATEGIC PROCESS TO DEVELOP DIVERSITY PLANS FOR SCHOOLS

Introduction

Some corporations have successfully adapted strategic management of diversity to their organizational contexts (Cox, 2000; Thomas, 1991). These strategic attempts have developed a level of structural integration that incorporates program, and process to establish a proactive strategic response (Dass & Parker, 1996). Effective management of diversity produces positive outcomes for organizations (Cox, 1993). When work force diversity is managed effectively, groups develop processes that enhance creativity, problem solving, team cohesiveness, and communication. Thus, organizational effectiveness will be improved, flexibility will be encouraged, and there will be a better recruitment of diverse workers (Cox, 1993). An innovative diversity strategy may involve a systematic process that includes visioning, nurturing, and adoption of new programs and processes. The question becomes, Will a strategic plan work for schools, and what adaptations need to be made for such a plan to operate successfully within a school context? In this chapter, we propose a strategic diversity plan as a way to address diversity-related issues and to improve organizational outcomes.

Leadership and the Implementation of a Diversity Plan

Individual organizations such as schools may achieve strategic advantage by targeting aspects of diversity that are most important for organizational achievement. Leaders can play a pivotal role in using a diverse work force to develop unique organizational strengths, add value to activities, and achieve an edge in attracting and retaining a diverse work force (Dass & Parker, 1996). We believe leadership is critical to the implementation of a diversity plan. Administrators need to cultivate the necessary conditions for determining the organizational direction for such a plan.

Before a diversity plan is considered, leaders must understand their own cultural identity and its relationship to others who are racially or ethnically different from them. By having this identity consciousness, leaders will be able to engage others in this process. They must recognize the significance of the identity orientations of their school participants in order to promote interpersonal cooperation and create dense and integrated networks. The development and implementation of an effective diversity plan must transcend the complex dynamics of race and ethnicity. Within this framework the leader needs to be the facilitator of dialogue for school inclusiveness.

In diverse contexts, it is critical to create an adaptable structure that evolves and expands as a diverse population comes through the school door. We believe that the tensions between the traditional structure and the development of participatory principles may be addressed through a strategic process. A diversity proposal assists leaders with ways to examine how the school recruits and retains teachers, socializes teachers upon their entry into a diverse context, and examines teaming structures to represent heterogeneous groupings. In addition, this process provides ways for administrators to motivate and reward individuals who work well with their diverse student population. A strategic effort is one approach that leaders may employ to remove barriers so that all individuals may become effective contributors within their schools.

Factors to Consider in Implementing a Diversity Plan

A number of factors must be taken into account for the development, implementation, and evaluation of a diversity plan. Research on diversity plans emphasizes that organizations need to have a very clear rationale for why the plan is important and how the process will improve organizational outcomes and effectiveness (Dass & Parker, 1996; Cox, 2001). Thus the primary consideration for a school is to have a *clearly articulated rationale* for the diversity plan and how it fits with the mission and values of the district. There must be a well-stated strategy to include diversity at all the levels of the decision-making process. More important, schools need to have a clear sense of the challenges they may face when ensuring involvement of all school participants in this strategic process.

School participants need to be conscious of the importance of *effective management of intergroup conflict.* In chapters 4 and 5, we noted how intergroup conflict, if not managed, may compromise efforts to create inclusive schools. Our findings clearly point to the important role of school leaders in creating inclusive school cultures. Additionally, Bell's (2002) study of European American teachers' and teachers of colors' perceptions of intergroup differences in urban schools demonstrates the importance of culture for teachers' decision-making processes. Thus, when implementing a strategic process, aspects of intergroup conflict must be addressed so they do not become organizational roadblocks that impede an inclusive process.

Other considerations are *education about or awareness of diversity.* The mere implementation of a diversity plan does not automatically imply that school participants will automatically accept group and individual differences. For sustainable results, there cannot be an espoused vision without consistent attention to the goals of diversity. The task of strategic integration requires meeting both organizational and individual outcomes. The diversity climate needs to be open to acculturation, not assimilation; acknowledgment of cultural variations; and an understanding that a strategic process may temporarily aggravate intergroup differences. Thus, the education or awareness phase means more than just lecturing about culturally relevant practices; it means engaging in active interactions among diverse groups of teachers to explore and develop pedagogical practices that will enhance the educational outcomes of *all* students. Ongoing professional development addressing culturally relevant concerns will become a necessity in order to constantly explore instructional practices and curricula that will enhance student outcomes.

Discussions about cultural differences are often laden with intense emotions and often based on individuals' experiences of prejudice and discrimination. These are deeply personal occurrences that must be acknowledged and handled with prudence, so as not to hinder the strategic process. If we are to deal with these emotion-laden concerns, there must be people who can facilitate discussions so individuals feel open to talk about race. As Cox (2001) notes, diversity work within a given organization requires layers of people who have true expertise on these issues. These highly skilled people should be selected from various levels of the organization and reflect multiple positions. More important, they should be individuals who can be *trusted* to smooth the progress of constructive dialogue across areas of difference.

Another factor is for schools to *foster diversity through targeting qualified people from underrepresented groups*. Cox (2001) asserts that three areas must be addressed to create a workplace environment where differences are valued: first, how diversity competence is assessed when job candidates apply; second, the composition of the recruitment and selection team; and third, how the organization educates its personnel about diversity issues. As noted in our discussion in chapters 2 and 3, there are significant implications if schools have only a handful of racial minority teachers who are frequently pigeonholed into particular roles and expected be the spokespersons only on issues related to diversity.

Another consideration is *how leaders are prepared* to address diversity-related issues. Leaders must have a sense of diversity self-efficacy if they are to begin the strategic process. Often, leaders are hesitant to address diversity issues because they may feel inadequately prepared to deal with racial undertones; they may not understand the complexity of intergroup differences; and/or they may have had only monocultural experiences, which may inhibit their ability to understand racial matters. The question of leader preparation requires us to think critically about the content of formal educational programs that prepare leaders for diverse contexts and about the value these individuals place on diversity.

When developing a strategic process for diversity, we need to reflect on ways to *assess diversity competency* within the following areas: assessment of performance appraisal, development of incentives to ensure that diversity practices are fulfilled, and the alignment of career development practices with goals of diversity. To ensure the success of a diversity plan, we need to examine institutional structures that motivate people to contribute to the attainment of the diversity goals. These are important elements for the creation of inclusive schools.

The preceding discussion highlights some of the factors that must be considered in implementing a diversity plan. See appendix D for an outline of the five phases of a strategic diversity plan.

Conclusion

We have worked with districts and schools in the early developmental stages of implementing a diversity plan. Interactions with school administrators indicated that in developing a strategic process, they became more aware of their student outcomes and made changes in the context of their school development plan. Schools must consider a long-term strategic advantage and develop a process throughout the organization to value differences. The development of a diversity plan involves an environmental scanning process to assess various perspectives so as to understand how people within the organization reflect on areas of diversity and to evaluate aspects of diversity in terms of personnel issues (Cox, 2001; Dass & Parker, 1996). Therefore, a strategic process offers a holistic approach and does not view diversity as segregated, but as inclusive through the development of a diversity plan (see appendix D).

Cox (2003) believes that research and measurement of organizational data answer questions about the environmental context in diversity-related matters. By examining data, schools will better understand how students of color are portrayed. For example, how many students of color are included in gifted programs, advanced placement (AP) classes, and other curriculum areas? What are the achievement discrepancies for all students? Does the number of teachers of color reflect the students' ethnicity? How many parents of color are included on advisory committees? While these questions seem relatively simplistic, many schools neglect to examine these data in the context of their diverse participants. Hence, the diversity plan must include a process for collecting comprehensive assessments and establish baseline data, benchmarking, and an evaluation process.

While we tend to focus more on ethnic and racial data collection for a diversity plan, schools may want to broaden this effort to include additional areas such as gender and sexual orientation. In addition, statistics reflect that many children in majority contexts must also be considered, so as to ensure their transition to a diverse world. A strategic process implementation should reflect what the schools define as diversity and how those areas can be measured, collected, and embedded in the school plan.

The diversity plan should also reflect an alignment between the district system and the school context. As noted earlier, this strategic diversity process has been developed for corporations, so we are hesitant to interpret how the alignment of the management systems in schools may be addressed. Cox (2003) believes that a strategic process should be embedded at all system levels of the organization. Therefore, we recommend that schools consider all aspects (noted above), such as human resource activities that include recruitment, promotion, and professional development opportunities; flexible work schedules; system outcomes; and levels of community and parent involvement outside the school context. All these aspects must be in alignment so that benchmarking and integration of goals can be measured.

Schools have to develop a process for evaluation to ensure the achievement of the diversity plan. For example: How will diversity plan outcomes be reported? How will changes to the plan be made? Who will be responsible for managing the process? How will the school address the benchmark areas for improvement? Follow-up and continual monitoring of the plan are important to ensure the completion of the diversity process. As the plan unfolds, we believe that schools must consider how diversity outcomes can be embedded in an ongoing school development (see appendix D).

There may not be one best strategy for all schools to create an inclusive response to diversity. Schools need to design their own strategies according to the types of diversity they choose to address and in response to their internal and external concerns. Therefore, having a strategic process focuses on redesigning organizational systems through a structural and cultural transformation that creates equity in these contexts. In responding to issues of diversity, it becomes important that a balanced atmosphere of homogeneity and heterogeneity be established in the form of a strategic process.

APPENDIX A
THE AFRICAN AMERICAN TEACHER AND SCHOOL LEADER STUDIES

We provide an overview of data collection, data analysis, and data sources for the findings we have presented in this book. Our findings are based on two separate studies that we conducted over a three-year period. The first study is a collection of interviews with African American male and female teachers in suburban desegregated schools. From our conversations with these teachers we gained insight into the complexity of their workplace relationships with their majority counterparts. We learned much about the performance pressures of being the sole person of color in an otherwise European American school. Problems of group boundaries emerged when teachers of color were expected to use traditional instructional patterns and when their ideas about teaching and other matters were not elicited except in matters having only to do with race, relegating them to the marginal role of "Black expert." We also learned that due to their minority status, these teachers became role entrapped and were not promoted to other leadership positions.

The second study is a more thorough overview of school participants' interviews and their interactions with African American teachers. We examined how teachers of color were perceived by European American teachers in these contexts and the implications for how the principals dealt with intergroup conflict. This second study was more comprehensive in that it allowed us to observe the instructional practices of European American and African American teachers; attend faculty meetings to observe both groups; and interview numerous teachers, parents, and principals in suburban desegregated contexts.

For both studies we used a case study methodology that dealt with suburban desegregated contexts. In our data analysis we employed a constant comparative method in which we used themes to compare the data with various research theories. For these two studies we used Kanter (1977), Cose (1993), intergroup conflict theory, and additional theoretical frames to code our findings. We used interviews, observations, and document analysis for data collection. We interviewed African American and European American teachers and school participants to ensure a good pool of interviewees. Therefore, the appendix will provide insights on how both studies were conducted, present a profile of the participants, describe the districts and school contexts, and explain the data analysis process.

Study I: The African American Teachers

Data Collection

For this first study we examined the workplace relationships of both male and female African American teachers in suburban desegregated schools. We defined a case study as a single entity, a unit of similar groups of people within the bounded context of suburban desegregated schools surrounding a midsize Midwest city (Merriam, 1998). Case studies are differentiated from other types of qualitative research in that they are intense descriptions and analyses of a single unit or bounded system (Smith, 1978). For this research we used a sampling of a setting (predominantly European American surburban desegregated schools) and the people of color who work in these contexts (Boyatzis, 1998) as the unit of analysis. African American teachers were identified because there is considerable literature on their pedagogy to make comparisons between African American and European American teachers (Foster, 1997; Hollins, 1982; Irvine, 1990; King, 1991).

We asked personnel directors from four desegregated suburban school districts surrounding a midsized Midwest city that participated in the city and county's voluntary desegregation plan if they would be willing to participate in this project. Those who agreed to do so provided the names, addresses, and phone numbers of all the African American teachers in their districts (see data sources section for more details of these districts). We invited all 21 teachers from the 4 districts to participate in this study; 14 responded positively. In our sample of 14 participants, we had an equal representation of males and females. We were specifically interested in the perceptions and experiences of the African American teachers in their interactions with school administrators, parents, and students.

Data Analysis

We employed a qualitative thematic strategy of data analysis to categorize and make judgments about the interpretation of the data. This methodological process became the unit of coding, and the participants' interviews became the unit of analysis and provided a theoretical justification, given the phenomenon of interest (Boyatzis, 1998). This analytical procedure allowed important themes and categories to emerge inductively from the data across schools and districts. We used the prior-research-driven approach to identify themes and to develop a coding process (Boyatzis, 1998). In establishing the reliability for this study, we analyzed the data using what Glaser and Strauss (1967) call a "constant comparative method." This process created a match between the interview data and the existing theory, and allowed the interplay between the data analysis and coding process as well.

This coding process was developed by comparing data from this study with Kanter's themes. Using her research and Cose's (1993) and Anderson's (1999), we preestablished a set of categories including performance pressures, group boundaries, and role entrapment. We were able to generate a data analysis code that could be applied to the participants' interview data (Boyatzis, 1998). By building on the aforementioned researchers' work, we were able to establish the theoretical framework to understand how suburban desegregated schools and their participants created problematic workplace relationships for teachers of color. These conceptually organized themes were clustered around related characteristics and the identification of an underlying construct (Boyatzis, 1998).

The findings from this study closely followed themes that evolved from Kanter's (1977) study of women in male-dominated corporations. Cultural switching, an additional theme not found in Kanter's work, was identified in this study. We consider this theme important in understanding cultural incongruence, in how the cultural norms of the African American female teachers differed from those of European American teachers. Pressured by these incongruences, the female African American teachers felt they had to "switch cultures" in response to public scrutiny of their actions. However, the African American male participants did not mention cultural switching in their interactions with their European American colleagues.

As a way to bring about a collective interpretation in the data analysis, we believed it was important for the reader to understand the complexities in collecting and analyzing cross-cultural research. Stanfield (1993) asserts that in race and ethnicity research, comparative analysis can be interpreted in a number of ways. He believes that researchers in mainstream disciplines rarely reflect on the effects of their own racial identities and how they influence their interpretations. It is also the norm in social sciences to assume that European American realities can be generalized to people of color. Stanfield (1993) further argues that there are ethical considerations in researching people of color because of cultural, class, and gender differences that require a special sensitivity.

In completing a collective interpretation of this cross-cultural study, a European American female completed the interviews with both the male and female African American teachers. However, the data analysis was a collaborative endeavor between the European American researcher and a scholar of African descent. For this study, each researcher analyzed the data separately to ensure a reliable coding system. Once the data were examined, we addressed different interpretations to ensure inter-rater reliability and a fair analysis of the African American teachers' reported perceptions of their schools. The two researchers held discussions about the differences in the cross-cultural interpretation of data in order to ensure a reliable and trustworthy interpretation of the findings (Merriam, 1998). Furthermore, there was a consistency of judgment between us to determine the code development and coding process (Boyatzis, 1998).

Although the pool of subjects was small, the participants' experiences and perceptions provided much commonality in terms of themes and findings. This study provides an in-depth look at patterns of experiences in a consistent type of suburban desegregated school to help us examine similar contextual configurations. We also believe that additional studies need to be conducted to disaggregate these participants' experiences so as to further define how the organizational structures of these contexts can be changed to prevent additional obstacles for teachers of color.

While the findings presented are based on the African American teachers' self-reports, these participants had taught for many years and had similar experiences across districts and schools in desegregated suburban contexts. Most of the African American males taught in secondary schools, while four of the female participants taught in elementary; the different grade levels may have influenced how these teachers responded to performance pressures. It is not the intent of the authors to represent and to perceive the European American teachers as one undifferentiated group, all of whom were similar in their relationships with the African American teachers. We are cognizant of the complexity that exists within these two groups and are cautious about portraying the European American teachers as a monolithic group. However, we are concerned about representing African American teachers' perceptions in a manner that captures their experiences in these schools.

Data Sources

Districts The study took place in four desegregated suburban districts surrounding a large Midwestern city that voluntarily chose to participate in the city's program. It is important to define culture of whiteness in these districts in order to provide a context for understanding the experiences of these African American teachers. Although these suburban desegregated districts were acclaimed for their academic superiority and resources, the neighboring inner-city public school did not share the same reputation. In their quest to receive what they perceived as a high-quality education, the inner-city students, the majority of whom were African American, participated in the interdistrict desegregation program. When the desegregation program was implemented in these districts, it was court mandated; however, now the program operates on a volunteer basis whereby students can elect to participate and withdraw. The wealthier suburban desegregated school districts where this study took place received additional funding for accepting the students from the city's inner-city schools. The overwhelming majority of the students and school participants in these districts were European American, with only a smattering of students of color and even fewer teachers and administrators of color.

The School Context The schools where our 14 participants taught were situated in 4 districts that were extensions of the more affluent metropolitan region. The schools were comparable in terms of student composition, resources, and size. They reflected the demographics of the districts in that they were predominantly European American, with only about 25 percent of the students from the city accepted through the desegregation program. African American teachers made up less than 4 percent of the faculty. To preserve the confidentiality and anonymity of the African American teachers who participated, the authors cannot provide a more detailed description of each participating school and district where this study was conducted. We believe that within these contexts there were similar conditions that can be generalized to similar contexts.

Profiles of the African American Teachers

Because of the limited number of African American teachers in these suburban desegregated school contexts, all African American participants who contacted the researcher were interviewed. While the pool of subjects was only 14, it became apparent throughout the data analysis that respondents had similar responses to performance pressures that affected their relationships with their European American colleagues. It is also important to note that the researcher did not contact those African Americans who chose not to participate in the project.

Male Teachers Seven African American male teachers were interviewed; 3 of them taught at the middle school and the other 4 taught at the high school. Two of the participants who taught at the middle school level had 6 to 7 years of experience at their school. While both of these African American participants had grown up in segregated environments, their experiences were different. One of them grew up in the South and attended segregated schools, while the other had lived in a segregated neighborhood in the city but attended a mostly European American private school.

The 4 oldest male African American participants were similar in years of experience and background. They had taught for approximately 20 to 30 years in their suburban desegregated districts. Most of them had had similar life experiences, growing up in segregated areas and then attending predominantly European American universities. The last participant, who had taught for 10 years at his high school, was the only African American at his school, while the other participants had taught with other African Americans at their schools. The participants' teaching experience ranged from 6 to 30 years. The group average was 18 years.

Female Teachers The 7 female African American teachers interviewed in this study varied in years of teaching in their schools. Only one had less than a year of teaching in a European American school. The two most experienced teachers had taught in their schools for 12 and 20 years, respectively. The other 4 participants had been with their schools for 5 to 10 years. For these 7 female participants, the average was 8.4 years teaching in the current context. Four of the teachers taught elementary grades, 2 were at the secondary level, and the other taught at the middle school. All of the teachers had attended historically Black colleges for their teacher preparation. Six had grown up in the African American community, and the other had lived in a suburban integrated neighborhood. Only a few of the participants had taught in urban schools where African American students were in the majority. Most of these participants' teaching experiences were in suburban desegregated schools.

The teachers stated that they came to these districts because they were committed to serving African American students who transferred there from the city's schools. They also felt that these districts paid well and there were resources that were not available to them in the city's schools.

Male Teachers: Gary Boyle grew up in the city but attended private schools in the suburbs that were predominantly European American. He studied at a European American university but eventually transferred to the city's historically Black college. He completed his student teaching in the city schools. He was offered an opportunity to teach in his present district. He has been with the district for 6 years.

Chester Burke grew up in the city and was educated in the city schools. He attended a European American state university, where he became certified as a business teacher. He has been with this district for the past 20 years. For approximately 3 years he was in the private sector, working in the city's major corporations. He was employed to adjust diversity issues in the workplace. He has developed a consulting business that does diversity training workshops.

Nathan Carson grew up in the rural South and attended segregated schools. After high school he joined the military and is still involved with the reserves. For his teacher preparation he studied at a historically Black institution. Prior to moving to his present district he taught in another mostly European American middle school. He has been with his district for over 7 years and is responsible for teaching the technology classes.

Wilson Grower grew up among the African American community in a rural area of the state. He attended a mostly European American state university. While there he joined an African American fraternity. He became certified as a math teacher and taught in the city's high school for 17 years. He was recruited by his present district to teach in the advanced placement math program. He has been with this district for the past 13 years.

Jason Inman grew up in the South and attended the segregated schools there. Family issues resulted in his moving to California and attending an integrated middle school. Eventually, he moved back to the South and attended a segregated high school. After high school he joined the military and became fluent in several languages. After his military experiences he joined the Peace Corps. After that he taught in the city schools before he was recruited by his present district. He has been with this district for the past 25 years.

Albert Lainson grew up in the South and attended predominantly African American schools. He attended an integrated high school. His college years were spent in a predominantly European American state university, where he took math and science courses. In 1965 he began teaching in his present district and has remained there for over 29 years.

Walter Richards grew up in the city and was educated in its schools. Upon completing high school, he entered a European American state university. He became certified as a math teacher at the high school level. He has been with his present district for 10 years.

Female Teachers: Sue Brown has spent most of her teaching career in European American schools. While she has been with this district for only 5 years, she previously taught in another European American district for 10 years. She, like the other participants, grew up in the city and attended the historically Black college. Prior to high school, she had little association with the European American community. She elected to teach in the district because of its progressive reputation and its salary and benefits. She has taught business education at the high school.

Sandi Davis attended a well-integrated private Catholic high school in the city. She grew up within the African American community and attended the historically Black college for her teacher preparation. The district hired her as a first grade teacher. She has been with the district for 12 years. She originally applied to the city schools but was informed there were no openings.

Jackie Jones was a veteran teacher who had taught in her European American district for 20 years. She taught in mostly European American schools before coming to this district. However, she grew up within the African American community and attended a historically Black college for her teacher preparation. She was a middle school math teacher. Her reason for remaining with the district was that it was close to her home and paid well.

Rita Morgan, like many of the other participants, grew up in the city and attended the historically Black college there. Her first teaching job was with this district, and she has remained for the past 6 years. She was the only African American teacher in her building and called her first year horrendous, but felt the need to remain at her school.

Julie Owens grew up in the African American community and attended the historically Black college for her teaching preparation. She had been with this district for 10 years, teaching at the elementary level. The district offered her the position after she had completed her student teaching.

Mary Rogers grew up in an integrated suburb near the city and attended school in mostly integrated settings. Her teaching degree was from the historically Black college, and she did her student teaching in the suburban districts. When she completed her student teaching, the district hired her to teach English at the secondary level.

Jane Smith is a first-year teacher in the district. She is a first grade teacher with little exposure to a European American school. She grew up in the African American community and attended the local historically Black college. Jane did her student teaching in the city and felt very comfortable about her teaching. She took the job because of the district's reputation and its salary scale for beginning teachers.

Study II: The School Leaders

Data Collection

The second study was a comprehensive qualitative case study (Merriam, 1998) that lasted throughout an entire school year in order to examine several areas: (1) the pedagogical practices of African American teachers in suburban desegregated schools, (2) the interactions between these teachers and European American teachers in responding to issues of diversity, and (3) the role of the principal in creating an inclusive school. Data collection methods included classroom observations that were completed weekly, attendance at multiple school and team meetings, and interviews of school participants. A total of 4 African American teachers, 21 European American teachers, 7 African American parents and 7 European American parents, 3 European American principals, and 4 African American assistant principals were interviewed. For this book, we focused on our interviews with the principals. We are in the process of analyzing the other data; therefore it was not included in this book.

Data collected for this study included intensive open-ended and follow-up interviews. Interviews took place at the respondents' schools. Additionally, some participants called us after the last interview to provide more thoughts and insights. As individual cases, these leaders shared their experiences, resulting in an interpretive study that sought out emic meanings held by these subjects (Stake, 1998). These interviews were extensive conversations that resulted in a well-triangulated case study.

The interview protocol consisted of 2 intensive open-ended interviews to further validate the participants' leadership in responding to intergroup conflict. The interview questions focused on the leaders' ability to act in response to issues of diversity, the procedures they used to recruit and retain teachers of color, and their role in leading school participants on issues of diversity. The interviews each lasted approximately 2 hours and were conducted at the middle and at the end of this research project. These interviews were taped and later transcribed for recurring themes. These leaders' interviews were used to focus the inquiry at the single case level of analysis (Merriam, 1988).

Data Analysis

We employed a qualitative thematic strategy of data analysis to categorize and make judgments about the interpretation of the data. This methodological process became the unit of coding for which the participants' responses could be assessed in a meaningful way. The participants' interviews became the unit of coding and provided a theoretical justification, given the phenomenon of interest and the unit of analysis (Boyatzis, 1998). We used the prior-research-driven approach to identify themes and to develop a coding process (Boyatzis, 1998). In establishing the reliability for this study, we analyzed the data using what Glaser and Strauss (1967) call a "constant comparative method." This process created a match between the interview data and the existing theory, and allowed interplay between the coding and data analysis as well. This coding process was constructed by comparing data from this study with the sources of intergroup conflict. Using the aforementioned researchers' preestablished set of categories of intergroup conflict, we were able to generate a data analysis code that we could apply to these participants' interview data (Boyatzis, 1998).

As a way to bring about a collective interpretation in the data analysis, we perceived it was important for readers to understand the complexities in collecting and analyzing cross-cultural research. Stanfield (1993) argues that there are ethical considerations in researching people of color and their contexts. In view of cultural, class, and gender differences, the collection and analysis of data require a special sensitivity. Furthermore, researchers in mainstream disciplines rarely reflect on how their racial identities influence their interpretations of data (Stanfield, 1993). Cross-cultural interpretations of data must be sensitive to issues of race since this may prohibit an appropriate interpretation of the findings.

The interpretation of the data was a joint effort between a European American and a colleague of African descent to ensure reliable and consistent cross-cultural analysis. Developing more inclusive ways to analyze data entails minority group members' insights about and interpretations of their experiences that are likely different from those of European American scholars (Anderson, 1999). This combined analysis was to ensure the validity and reliability of this qualitative study. In this cross-cultural analysis each researcher analyzed and coded data separately to protect the trustworthiness of the data. We had extensive discussions about the coding differences in the cross-cultural interpretations of these participants' experiences as a way to establish a reliable and trustworthy interpretation of the findings (Merriam, 1988). Furthermore, there was a consistency of judgment between us to determine code development and its application to data analysis (Boyatzis, 1998).

The findings from this study indicate that the leaders' leadership patterns in these suburban desegregated schools ought to be applicable only to similar contextual configurations. These were older homogeneous suburban desegregated schools that were experiencing population increases due to the city's desegregation plan and changing demographics. Thus, there was a blending of a school-age population that was not entirely European American. These administrators' perceptions and practices in managing issues of diversity provided a commonality in terms of themes and findings that may be generalized only to these types of contexts. Thus, additional study in urban and rural contexts may elicit other leadership responses to intergroup conflict among and between minority and majority teachers.

Districts and Schools The participating suburban desegregated elementary school was part of a district that was a member of a Midwest city's voluntary desegregation program. This district accepted less than 25 percent of its minority students from a court-mandated desegregation program, and the number of teachers of color amounted to less than 2 percent of the teaching staff. The school where the European American teachers were interviewed had 2 African American teachers (at the third and fifth grade levels). The elementary school was organized into grade-level teams with 4 to 5 teachers on a team. Teachers on these teams taught specific subject areas and were given in-school time to meet daily to address curriculum and student issues. The third and fifth grade teams each had an African American teacher. It is important to note that the European American teachers spent considerable time interacting with these African American teachers in a team process to make grade-level decisions. We interviewed the 7 European American teachers from these 2 teams.

Profiles of the School Leaders

European American School Leaders: Jane Frank had been in her district for most of her teaching career. Jane believed that her district was committed to issues of diversity, and she often took on the role of searching for teachers of color. She had moved through the ranks from teacher to principal in her school. She had been a principal for over 8 years. During the interview, she spoke about the high quality of the 2 African American teachers in her school. Jane also noted that she often sought the advice of the veteran African American teacher to ask her about issues of diversity, placement of African American students, and parent issues in dealing with multicultural concerns. She stated that she did not view herself as a school administrator because she truly felt that she was an educator. She defined her leadership vision as being concerned with issues of equity and social justice. Jane believed that the voluntary desegregation program had had a significant impact on her personally and on the community. Jane believed that the desegregation program "forced them to look at things that otherwise this little white community never would have looked at." Jane stated that the school's staff development program was not adequate to prepare the school for issues of diversity. She also mentioned the tensions among her groups of teachers that existed when issues of race become apparent in African American students' placements and in discussions about hiring teachers of color.

Mary Jones was in the same district as Jane, but her school was located in another part of the district. Unlike Jane Frank, Mary did not see diversity concerns as important because she believed the focus for her school should be to promote technology. Mary had worked as a resource room teacher prior to becoming the principal. She has been a principal for 3 years and taught alongside the African American teacher prior to becoming the school administrator. Mary had mixed emotions about the African American teacher in her building. While she believed that the African American teacher was excellent, she stated that this teacher was unwilling to assume any leadership responsibilities for her grade-level meeting. Much like Jane Frank, Mary stated that she often talked with the African American teacher about multicultural concerns and how to work with African American parents. Mary felt that she had a mostly middle-class background and admitted that she had had limited exposure to people of color. Mary felt there were tensions in the building due to the district's commitment to hiring teachers of color. Mary was uncomfortable with how to hire teachers of color and was hesitant to provide leadership to the hiring team. She stated that she often placed the African American teacher on the hiring team so this teacher could provide that expertise.

Susan James was in a larger suburban district than the other 2 leaders. Like them, she had been a teacher in the district before becoming a school administrator. She had been leading her school for the past 9 years. In her building there were two African American teachers. However, only the male African American teacher participated in this research project. Susan noted that her personnel director had played an important role in recruiting teachers of color to the district. Unlike the other 2 leaders, Susan did not seek out the 2 African American teachers on multicultural issues. She also noted that the school's African American teachers were excellent and well regarded by parents. Susan told of several glowing reports that she had received about the male African American teacher at her school. However, much like the other 2 leaders, she felt that these teachers needed to assume a greater leadership role in working with their European American colleagues. Susan, like the other leaders, was concerned about the African American teachers' self-imposed isolation and was unable to understand why these teachers did not attend social activities. She felt the school should hire the "best candidate," and that did not always translate into being concerned with issues of diversity. She believed it was the district's function to recruit teachers of color and not the principal's place.

African American School Leaders: Roger Winter grew up in an urban neighborhood and attended an integrated school until the fifth grade. Elementary school was an academically successful experience for him because the competition in his classes kept him focused on his studies. Upon completion of his elementary schooling, he was bused to a predominantly homogeneous European American school. During high school, he experienced positive interactions and friendships with European American students. Upon graduation, he pursued his baccalaureate studies at a predominantly European American university. He studied journalism in college and became a sportswriter for a local paper upon graduation. After several years, he became "tired of this position." In his quest to "give back and work with African American children," Mr. Winter explored the possibility of coaching or substitute teaching. However, he was unable to secure a position in these areas. The personnel director recruited Mr. Winter to teach in a suburban school district. After teaching high school English for approximately 6 years, he was invited to apply for an administrator position where he would be responsible for student management. While he has played an important role in assisting African American students to navigate the maze of desegregated schooling, Mr. Winter expressed concerns about his own future in the district, especially opportunities for promotion.

Ralph Green was the only elementary assistant principal participating in this study. He received his elementary and high school education at mostly European American schools. After completing high school, Mr. Green joined the military and remained there for 4 years. After his military experience, he attended a historically Black institution, where he received his teacher preparation. Mr. Green began his teaching career in his current suburban school district. He taught in the district for 12 years before he was invited to apply for an assistant principal position at another school within the district. Mr. Green's responsibilities include student discipline, staff development, and community outreach. Like the other participants, he hopes to be an elementary principal in the near future.

David Main attended one of the most recognized preparatory high schools in the city. After completing high school he enrolled at a predominantly European American university, where he acquired his teacher preparation. Upon his graduation from the university, Mr. Main applied for a teaching position at several suburban districts. He eventually took a position with one of the most prestigious suburban districts. After 2 years of teaching he completed his master's degree in school administration. Although Mr. Main characterized himself as an excellent teacher, his ultimate goal was to be a school administrator. Therefore, after 3 years of teaching he made the decision to leave the classroom. He interviewed in another suburban district for an assistant principal position at the high school level. Mr. Main was offered the position, which he had held for 2 years. He believes the principal at his high school has become his mentor.

Maxine Boyd grew up in the rural South and attended mostly segregated schools. She said that she never had a white teacher until she entered college. She believed that African American teachers were important for her success and attributed their support to her aspiration to be a teacher. She attended a historically Black college, where she received her baccalaureate degree in teaching. Upon graduation, she taught for 2 years in a rural community, but soon became weary of teaching in a poverty-stricken area. She followed her family members to this city as part of the northern "Black migration." She obtained a teaching position in the city's schools and ascended through the ranks to become an administrator. When the city implemented a policy that all administrators had to reside within the city limits (where she did not live), Ms. Boyd took a position in the suburban schools after 25 years of working in urban schools. She accepted a high school assistant principal position with a highly recognized suburban district. At the time of this study, Ms. Boyd had been in this position for 3 years. She noted that in her current administrative position, she spent most of her time with the "deseg" children who transferred to her district from the city schools. Ms. Boyd struggled with how other administrators perceived her. She believed that there was an expectation that she was responsible for the African American students in her school. While she enjoyed her role in the school, she often became tired of the stereotypes confronting her on a daily basis. Of all of the participants, she alone noted the strains of feeling "out of place," yet needing to be there for the African American students.

APPENDIX B
PROPERTIES OF INTERGROUP CONFLICT

Competing Goals: Differences among majority and minority workers result in competing goals that are influenced by norms, goal priorities, and work styles among and between these groups (Cox, 1994).

Competition for Resources: Allocation of resources produces competition when it is influenced by embedded organizational issues such as acknowledgment of group identities in regulating jobs, training priorities, and expansion of resources (Cox, 1994).

Cultural Differences: Cultural differences between members of different groups occur due to misunderstanding and misperceptions (Cox, 1994).

Power Differences: Majority groups hold advantages over minority groups in the power structure of the organization. Hostility between groups results in a disagreement over the redistribution of power. Minority group density in organizations poses a threat to the existing power structure and provides an opportunity for those who are powerless.

The types of resources that can be obtained and used differ among groups (Cox, 1994; Alderfer & Smith, 1982).

Conformity versus Identity Affirmation: This is the tension between majority and minority group members over the preservation of minority group identity (Cox, 1994).

Group Boundaries: Both physical and psychological group boundaries determine group membership. Transactions among groups are regulated by variations in the permeability of the boundaries (Alderfer & Smith, 1982).

Affective Patterns: The severity of intergroup conflict is related to the degree to which feelings among the groups are polarized. Group members split their feelings so that positive feelings are associated with their group and negative feelings are associated with other groups (Alderfer & Smith, 1982).

Cognitive Formations: Due to group boundaries, power differences, and affective patterns, group members develop their own language, influence members' perceptions of subjective and objective criteria of other groups and work efforts, and transmit propositions about other groups in relation to their own group members (Alderfer & Smith, 1982).

Leadership Behavior: The group leader reflects the boundaries of groups and how they will interact. Members of a similar group reflect power differences, affective patterns, and cognitive formations of their group in relation to the other groups. The role of the leader in a network of intergroup relations determines the intensification of intergroup conflict (Alderfer & Smith, 1982; Alderfer, 1977).

APPENDIX C
LEADERSHIP COMPETENCIES FOR DIVERSE CONTEXTS

Understands and Challenges Racial Boundaries

Understands the intercultural connections among ethnic groups and envisions systemic variations in how school participants see themselves as connected to their own ethnic group; also understands how diversity at the individual level affects differences at the group level.

Understands how racial identification creates categorization for students

Understands sense of otherness, such as skin color, language, accent, cultural performances

Examines self and understands how school participants assign identity

Understands racial boundary formation

Understands that racial boundaries should not be fixed, and are in flux due to social interactions in which identities are produced or reproduced

Understands racial meaning, power, and exclusion

Racial identifications are not just thought processes but also actions, so leader prevents acts of exclusion

Understands how the school is influenced by a diverse constituency

Understands how school with its diverse participants has a set of dynamics, rules, and cultural repertoires

Understands how school context shapes not only how we think about others, but also how and whether we think about our own racial identities

Challenges Racial Boundaries

Challenges the racial boundaries of the school and community to ensure all are treated equitably

Develops an Organizational Identity and Responds to Image Management

Leader promotes a collective understanding of core values and beliefs that translates into actions of responsiveness to diverse constituencies

Retains core beliefs and identity

Establishes a culture that institutes the school's image as being responsive to issues of diversity

Models and directs the core beliefs about being responsive to the diversity of the school participants

Overcomes district roadblocks in establishing a school's identity

Provides outreach to community and models appropriate responses to diversity

Establishes a process to understand how the school is perceived

Works with teachers to ensure they understand how the parents' perceptions of the schools have implications for their school's success

Understands the interrelationship between image and organizational identity, and its implications for creating a leadership style that adapts to these destabilizing forces

Puts needs of children in the context of their culture

Works with teachers to establish appropriate strategies for diverse learners

Establishes professional development opportunities to support teachers in their understanding of diversity

Ensures that teachers support a relational identity orientation in classrooms

Creates an internal school culture that supports outreach and positive school image

Supports working families through various school activities

Creates family-sponsored activities

Engages parents from all ethnic groups and reflects school population

Provides families with language support and bicultural issues

Creates a Relational Identity Orientation

Has a strong understanding of the importance of the identity orientation of school participants and its implications for creating a relational orientation that will promote an interpersonal cooperation to create relationship partners in educating a diverse school population

Interpersonal cooperation: Leader creates an environment where there is a collectivist perspective in addressing issues of diversity

Requires teachers to relate to all students collectively and individually

Hires and promotes teachers who are aware of diversity and sensitive to identity

Works with teachers to ensure that they use a relational identity orientation

Dense and integrated networks: Leader establishes an organization to create relational partnerships among school participants to promote "other" relationship

Supports teachers in discussing their life experiences in areas of diversity

Addresses concerns about biases and equity for all school participants

Leads discussions with teachers about their instructional practices
and their implications for improving student outcomes

Challenges biases and works through racial undertones

Supports others' interest versus self-interest: Leader ensures a collectivist perspective
in which the cultural identities of all school participants are promoted

Nurtures teachers and their own sense of cultural identity and its
implications for working with students

Encourages risk-taking with teachers in their interactions with
students of color

Mentors teachers in their journey on diversity issues

Supports teachers who choose to remain in diverse contexts

Creates interindividual/interpersonal attachment: Leader establishes opportunities
for exchange among groups to form interpersonal attachments

Assumes that being from a minority group does not automatically
imply that you have an attachment to students from other ethnic
groups

Surrounds teams and groups of teachers with those who have positive beliefs about students of color

Encourages teachers to share their frustrations about working in
urban contexts

Establishes high expectations for all students and encourages
teachers to do the same

Creates supportive environment for teachers to share and learn
from each other

Develops an Adaptive Organizational Structure

Establishes an organizational structure that creates a relationship
between followers and leader to accomplish organizational goals, thus
forming an adaptive structure that requires participants to be flexible in
working with diverse group of students

Creates an adaptive organizational structure: Leader reorganizes the
organizational structure for adaptability in response to diverse student population

Creates an organization that is flexible and dynamic, so that it
continually evolves and expands

Creates an interrelationship between building relationships of
school participants and tasks to be accomplished

Understands the tensions between the traditional structure and
the need to establish participatory principles

*Creates group processes that understand the dynamics of group interactions and
group decision making*

Helps school participants to follow specific participatory processes designed to improve outcomes and efficiency

Understands the precariousness of individual versus group dimensions in the day-to-day negotiations of communication, organization, role, and identity

Facilitates the ability to differentiate between mainstream culture
and other cultures in the school

*Establishes different approaches for motivating school participants in order to keep
them committed to educating students of color*

Appropriate compensation, equitable parity, use of physical space,
multiple dimensions of rewards, and performance development

*Deals with community/institutional conflict in a manner that empowers/involves
school and community participants*

Develops formal and informal networks with community to
engage their participation

Appendix D
Strategic Response to Diversity

Phase I

    Leadership and commitment to strategic process

Phase II

    Data analysis
    Assessment of organizational outcomes
    Development of diversity goals and their incorporation into the
      district and school plans

Phase III

    Implementation
    Development of a process to assess and develop diversity goals

Phase IV

    Integration
    Develop monitoring and organizational structure to ensure inte-
      gration of goals and objectives

Phase V

Evaluation and continuous assessment

Evaluation of goal implementation and staff commitment

PHASE I Leadership and Commitment to Strategic Process

Assisting people to see the critical need to make the link between meeting the academic needs of students of color and diversity goals

Helping people to see that the school must expand its outreach to students of color, given projected demographics

Developing a task force of various cultural and social backgrounds to develop a strategic perspective at the district and school levels

Encouraging people formally and informally to become "color-conscious" rather than "color-blind," in order to prevent inter-group conflict

Leadership capacity to address issues of diversity and their implications for administering the diversity plan in areas of organizational direction and image perceptions, development of a relational identity orientation among and between groups, development of a flexible organizational structure that adapts to the needs of teachers and students

PHASE II Data Analysis: Collecting Baseline Data and Benchmarking at the District and School Levels

Examine sources for data collection, such as state measures, school and district data, community statistics

Begin the process of collecting and assessing school and district data

Considerations for Collecting

Personnel Practices Number of teachers of color and leaders of color in relation to number of students and students of color, paraprofessionals; review of recruitment practices and hiring procedures

Staff Development Teacher needs in responding to students of color, sharing of instructional practices that meet the needs of students

of color, development of leadership initiatives to support principals in these contexts

Multicultural Awareness Analysis of curriculum, textbooks, selection of
library books, multicultural awareness, celebrations, cultural traditions, course offerings

Parent and Community Involvement Percentage of parents of color on
school/district committees, attendance, programs, community
outreach, advisory boards

Students of Color Disaggregate achievement levels, dropout and
mobility rates, attendance, discipline referrals, management
practices, support systems, number of students of color in special
education, gifted courses, advanced placement classes, higher-
division math and science courses, bilingual needs, after-school
programs

School Organization and Staffing Structure for diversity, heterogeneous
versus homogeneous teaming, school collaboration opportunities, leadership concerns in promoting diversity, socialization of
teachers into diverse contexts, mentoring, leaders of color on
teams

Organizational Culture: Community and Image Issues Supportive environment that allows expression of differences, development of
questionnaires/surveys to assess overall impressions in response
to diversity, establishment of process that creates inclusiveness,
addressing image issues related to diversity within the school
and community

**PHASE III Implementation, Development of Diversity Goals in School and
District Plan**

Parental Involvement

Based on your data, explain why these three goals are important,
how they will promote diversity in the school and be implemented, and how these factors will be measured

Curriculum and Instructional Practices Based on your data, explain why these three goals are important, how will they promote diversity in the school and be implemented, and how these factors will be measured

Staff Development Based on your diagnosis, explain why these three goals are important, how they will promote diversity in the school and be implemented, and how these factors will be measured

School Reorganization and Staffing Teaming and Collaboration: Based on your diagnosis, explain why these three goals are important, how they will promote diversity in the school and be implemented and how they will be measured

Students of Color Based on your diagnosis, explain why these three goals are important, how they will promote diversity in the school and be implemented, and how they will be measured

Support Systems Based on your diagnosis, explain why these three goals are important, how will they promote diversity in the school and be implemented, and how they will be measured

PHASE IV Integration Process

Develop incentives to implement diversity goals
Identify individuals who have leadership skills and expertise in the area of diversity to collect and assess data
Use integration phase to ensure the process is working

PHASE V Evaluation

Develop a continuous monitoring structure to evaluate diversity goals
Develop a benchmarking process that will be embedded in student achievement, job satisfaction, and commitment to the organization

References

Albert, S., & Whetten, D. (1985). Organizational identity. In L. L. Cummings & B. M. Staw (Eds.), *Research in organizational behavior, 7*, 263–295. Greenwich, CT: JAI Press.

Alderfer, C. P. (1977). Group and intergroup relations. In J. R. Hackman & J. L. Suttle (Eds.), *Improving life at work* (pp. 277–296). Santa Monica, CA: Goodyear.

Alderfer, C. P., Alderfer, C. J., Tucker, L., & Tucker, R. (1980). Diagnosing race relations in management. *Journal of Applied Psychology, 16*, 135–166.

Alderfer, C. P., & Smith, K. K. (1982). Studying intergroup relations embedded in organizations. *Administration Science Quarterly, 27*(1), 36–65.

Anderson, E. (1999). The social situation of the black executive: Black and white identities in the corporate world. In Michele Lamont (Ed.), *The cultural territories of race: Black and white boundaries* (pp. 3–29). Chicago: University of Chicago Press.

Ayman, R. (1993). Leadership perceptions: The role of gender and culture. In M. Chemers & R. Ayman (Eds.), *Leadership theory and research: Perspectives and directions* (pp. 137–166). San Diego, CA: Academic Press.

Bass, B. M. (1985). *Leadership and performance beyond expectations.* New York: Free Press.

Bell, E. L. (1990). The bicultural life experience of career-oriented Black women. *Journal of Organizational Behavior, 11*, 459–477.

Bell, S. (2002). Teachers' perceptions of intergroup conflict in urban schools. *Peabody Journal of Education, 77*(1), 59–81.

Berstein, D. (1984). *Company image and reality: A critique of corporate communications.* Eastbourne, UK: Holt, Rinehart & Winston.

Boyatzis, R. (1998). *Transforming qualitative information: Thematic analysis and code development.* Thousand Oaks, CA: Sage.

Brewer, M. B. (1991). The social self: On being the same and different at the same time. *Personality and Social Psychology Bulletin, 17*, 475–482.

Brewer, M. B., & Gardener, W. (1996). Who is this "we"? Levels of collective identity and self representations. *Journal of Personality and Social Psychology, 71*, 83–93.

Brewer, M. B., & Miller, N. (1984). Beyond the contact hypothesis: Theoretical perspectives on desegregation. In N. Miller & M. B. Brewer (Eds.), *Group in contact: The psychology of desegregation* (pp. 281–302). New York: Academic Press.

Brickson, S. (2000). The impact of identity orientation on individual and organizational outcomes in demographically diverse settings. *Academy of Management Review, 25*(1), 82–101.

169

Butler, J. (1976). Inequality in the military: An examination of promotion time for black and white enlisted men. *American Sociological Review, 41,* 807–818.

Chemers, M. (1993). An integrative theory of leadership. In M. Chemers & R. Ayman (Eds.), *Leadership theory and research: Perspective and directions* (pp. 239–319). San Diego, CA: Academic Press.

Chemers, M. M., & Murphy, S. E. (1995). Leadership and diversity in group and organizations. In M. M. Chemers, S. Oskamp, & M. A. Costanzo (Eds.), *Diversity in organizations: New perspectives for a changing workplace* (pp. 157–190). Thousand Oaks, CA: Sage.

Chemers, M., Oskamp, S., & Costanzo, M. (Eds.). (1995). *Diversity in organizations: New perspectives for a changing workplace.* Thousand Oaks, CA: Sage.

Chen, C., & Van Velsor, E. (1996). New directions for research and practice in diversity leadership. *Leadership Quarterly, 7*(2), 285–302.

Combs, G. (2002). Meeting the leadership challenges of a diverse and pluralistic workplace: Implications of self-efficacy for diversity training. *Journal of Leadership Studies, 8*(4), 1–16.

Cooley, C. H. (1902). *Human nature and the social order.* New York: Scribner's.

Cose, E. (1993). *The rage of a privileged class.* New York: HarperCollins.

Cox, T. (1993). *Cultural diversity in organizations: Theory, research, and practice.* San Francisco: Berrett-Koehler.

Cox, T. (1994). *Cultural diversity in organizations: Theory, research, and practice.* San Francisco: Berrett-Koehler.

Cox, T. (2001). *Creating the multicultural organization: A strategy for capturing the power of diversity.* San Francisco: Jossey-Bass.

Cross, W., Strauss, L., & Fhagen-Smith, P. (1999). African American development across the life span: Educational implications. In R. Sheets & E. Hollins (Eds.), *Racial and ethnic identity in school practices* (pp. 29–39). Mahwah, NJ: Lawrence Erlbaum Associates.

Dass, P., & Parker, B. (1996). Diversity: A strategic issue. In E. E. Kossek & S. A. Lobel (Eds.), *Managing diversity: Human resources strategies for transforming the workplace.* Cambridge, MA: Blackwell.

Dickens, F., Jr., & Dickens, J. B. (1991). *The black manager: Making it in the corporate world.* New York: American Management Association.

DiTomaso, N., & Hooijberg, R. (1996). Diversity and the demands of leadership. *Leadership Quarterly, 7*(2), 163–187.

Dovido, J. F., Gaertner, S. I., & Bachman, B. A. (2001). Racial bias in organizations: The role of group processes in its causes and cures. In M. E. Turner (Ed.), *Groups at work: Theory and research* (pp. 415–470). Mahwah, NJ: Lawrence Erlbaum Associates.

Ferdman, B. M. (1995). Cultural identity and diversity in organizations: Bridging the gap between group differences and individual uniqueness. In M. M. Chemers, S. Oskamp, & M. A. Costanzo (Eds.), *Diversity in organizations: New perspectives for a changing workplace* (pp. 37–61). Thousand Oaks, CA: Sage.

Fombrun, C. J. (1996). *Reputation: Realizing value from the corporate image.* Boston: Harvard Business School Press.

Foster, M. (Ed.). (1997). *Black teachers on teaching.* New York: New Press.

Frierson, H. T. (1990). The situation of Black educational researchers: Continuation of a crisis. *Educational Research, 19*(2), 12–18.

Gioa, D. A., Schultz, M., & Corley, K. G. (2000). Organizational identity, image, and adaptive instability. *Management Review, 1,* 63–81.

Glaser, B., & Strauss, A. (1967). *The discovery of grounded theory: Strategies for qualitative research.* Chicago: Aldine.

Gordon, J. (2000). *The color of teaching.* New York: Routledge Falmer.

Graen, G., & Uhl-Bien, M. (1995). Development of leader–member exchange (LMX) theory of leadership over 25 years: Applying a multi-level-multi-domain perspective. *Leadership Quarterly, 6,* 219–247.

Grant, C., & Sleeter, C. (1989). *Turning on learning: Five approaches for multicultural teaching plans for race, class, gender, and disability.* Columbus, OH: Merrill.

Greenhaus, J., Parasuraman, S., & Wormley, W. (1990). Effects of race on organizational experiences, job performance evaluations, and career outcomes. *Academy of Management Journal, 33,* 64–86.

Hollins, E. R. (1982). The Marva Collins story revisited. *Journal of Teacher Education, 33*(1), 37–40.

Irvine, J. J. (1990). *Black children and school failure: Policies, practices and prescriptions.* Westport, CT: Greenwood Press.

Jablin, F. M. (1987). Organizational entry, assimilation, and exit. In F. Jablin, L. L. Putnam, K. H. Roberts, & L. W. Porter (Eds.), *Handbook of organizational communication: An interdisciplinary perspective* (pp. 679–740). Newbury Park, CA: Sage.

Kanter, R.M. (1977). Some effects of proportions on group life: Skewed sex ratios and responses to token women. *American Journal of Sociology, 82*(5), 965–990.

King, J. (1991). Black student alienation and black teachers' emancipatory pedagogy. In M. Foster (Ed.), *Readings on equal education: Qualitative investigations in schools and schooling,* (pp. 245–217). New York: AMS Press.

Kossek, E. E., & Lobel, S. A. (1996). *Managing diversity: Human resources strategies for transforming the workplace.* Cambridge, MA: Blackwell.

Ladson-Billings, G. (1994). *The dreamkeepers: Successful teachers of African American children.* San Francisco: Jossey-Bass.

Lewis, A. (2001). There is no "race" in the schoolyard: Color-blind ideology in an (almost) all-white school. *American Educational Research Journal, 38*(4), 781–811.

Lewis, A. (2003). *Race in the schoolyard: Negotiating the color line in classrooms and communities.* New Brunswick, NJ: Rutgers University Press.

Livers, A. B., & Carver, K. A. (2003). *Leading in black and white: Working across the racial divide in corporate America.* San Francisco: Jossey-Bass.

Mabokela, R. O., & Madsen, J. A. (2003a). Crossing boundaries: African American teachers in suburban schools. *Comparative Education Review, 47*(1), 90–111.

Mabokela, R. O., & Madsen, J. A. (2003b). Intergroup differences and their impact on African American teachers. *Urban Education, 38*(6), 725–749.

Madsen, J. A., & Mabokela, R. O. (2000). Organizational culture and its impact on African American teachers. *American Educational Research Journal, 37*(4), 781–811.

Madsen, J. A., & Mabokela, R. O. (2002). African American leaders' perceptions of intergroup conflict. *Peabody Journal of Education, 77*(1), 35–58.

Merriam, S. (1988). *Case study research in education: A qualitative approach.* San Francisco: Jossey-Bass.

Merriam, S. (1998). *Qualitative research and case study applications in education.* San Francisco: Jossey-Bass.

Miller, J., Labovitz, S., & Fry, L. (1975). Inequities in the organizational experiences of women and men. *Social Forces, 54,* 365–381.

Miller, J., Lincoln, J., & Olson, J. (1981). Rationality and equity in professional networks: Gender and race as factors in the stratification of interorganizational systems. *American Journal of Sociology, 82*(2), 87–96.

Morrison, A. M. (1996). *The new leaders: Leadership diversity in America.* San Francisco: Jossey-Bass.

Nicoteria, A. M., Clinkscales, M. J., & Walker, F. R. (2003). *Understanding organization through culture and structure.* Mahwah, NJ: Lawerence Erlbaum Associates.

Nkomo, S., & Cox, T. (1996). Diverse identities in organizations. In S. Clegg, C. Hardy, & W. Nord (Eds.), *Handbook of Organization Studies*. (pp. 338–356). Thousand Oaks, CA: Sage.

Orbe, M. (1998). *Constructing co-cultural theory*. Thousand Oaks, CA: Sage.

Parker, P. S., & Ogilvie, D. (1996). Gender, culture, and leadership: Toward a culturally distinct model of African-American women executives' leadership strategies. *Leadership Quarterly, 7*(2), 189–214.

Porter, A. C., & Brophy, J. (1988). Synthesis of research on good teaching: Insights from the work of the Institute for Research on Teaching. *Educational Leadership, 45*(8), 74–85.

Ragins, B. R. (1995). Diversity, power, and mentorship in organizations: A cultural, structural, and behavioral perspective. In M. M. Chemers, S. Oskamp, & M. A. Costanzo (Eds.), *Diversity in organizations: New perspectives for a changing workplace* (pp. 91–132). Thousand Oaks, CA: Sage.

Ransford, H., & Miller, J. (1983). Race, sex, and feminist outlooks. *American Sociological Review, 48,* 46–59.

Riehl, C. J. (2000). The principal's role in creating inclusive schools for diverse students: A review of normative, empirical, and critical literature on the practice of educational administration. *Review of Educational Research, 70*(1), 55–88.

Scofield, J. W. (1989). *Black and white in schools*. New York: Teachers College Press

Scott, W. (1983). Trust differences between men and women in superior–subordinate relationships. *Group and Organizational Studies, 8,* 319–336.

Smart, J. C., & St. John, E. P. (1996). Organizational culture and effectiveness in higher education: A test of the Culture Type and Strong Culture Hypotheses. *Educational Education and Policy Analysis, 18*(3), 219–241.

Smith, L. M. (1978). An evolving logic of participant observation, educational ethnography and other case studies. In L. Shulman (Ed.), *Review of Research in Education*. Itasca, IL: Peacock.

Stake, R. E. (1998). Case studies. In N. Denzin & Y. Lincoln (Eds.), *Strategies of Qualitative Inquiry*. (pp. 86–109). Thousand Oaks, CA: Sage.

Stanfield, J. H. II (1993). Epistemological considerations. In J. H. Stanfield II & D. M. Rutlege (Eds.), *Race and ethnicity in research methods* (pp. 16–39). Newbury Park, CA: Sage.

Thomas, R. (1991). *Beyond race and gender: Unleashing the power of your total work force by managing diversity*. New York: AMACOM.

Thomas, R. (1996). *Redefining diversity*. New York: American Management Association.

Triandis, H. C. (1995). A theoretical framework for the study of diversity. In M. M. Chemers, S. Oskamp, & M. A. Costanzo (Eds.), *Diversity in organizations* (pp. 11–36). Thousand Oaks, CA: Sage.

Verdugo, R., Greenburg, N., Henderson, R., Uribe, O., & Schneider, J. (1997). School governance regimes and teachers' job satisfaction: Bureaucracy, legitimacy, and community. *Educational Administration Quarterly, 1*(33). 38–66.

Watts, R. J. (1994). Paradigms of diversity. In E. J. Trickett, R. J. Watts, & D. Birnam (Eds.), *Human diversity: Perspectives on people in context* (pp. 49–81). San Francisco: Jossey-Bass.

Wells, A. S., & Crain, R. L. (1997). *Stepping over the color line: African American students in white suburban schools*. New Haven, CT: Yale University Press.

Index